SETTING YOUR COURSE:

The Foundation For Success

SETTING YOUR COURSE:
The Foundation For Success

Harrison House
Tulsa, Oklahoma

All scripture text is taken from the King James Version unless otherwise specified with permission granted as stated below.

Scripture quotations from Amplified New Testament, Copyright The Lockman Foundation 1954, 1958

ISBN 0-931697-04-2

Copyright © 1984 by Casey Douglas Treat
Printed in the U.S.A. 1985
All rights reserved.

Published by Casey Treat Ministries
P.O. Box 98581
Seattle, Wa 98188

Table of Contents

Foreword

Dedication

Introduction by Dr. Lester Sumrall

Preface

Foreword

This book is not a lot of theological jargon or doctrinal essays. It will give you a simple view of the basic elements of the Christian faith and life. My prayer is that you will be strengthened as you understand the basics of the Bible and the first steps to success.

II Timothy 3:16,17 says: "All scripture is given by inspiration of God, and is profitable for doctrine, for reproof, for correction, for instruction in righteousness: That the man of God may be perfect, thoroughly furnished unto all good works." It is God's desire that all people "profit" spiritually, mentally, and physically, and that we be successful in every good work.

Through the Word of God you will gain the knowledge to be a winner in every realm of life. The lessons in this book will give you a strong foundation on which to stand firmly. Jesus said when you hear and do His Word you are building your house on the rock. I pray this message will help you to build a prosperous life on a solid foundation.

Casey Treat

DEDICATION

This book is dedicated to all the members of Christian Faith Center who have given themselves to Jesus and to the world. They are givers and workers of the Kingdom of God. Their faith and love have changed my life and thousands of lives around the world.

INTRODUCTION

I am thankful for the spiritual vision and delightful energy of Pastor Casey Treat. His growth in God's Word and church development are reassuring. It is very easy to grow in knowledge of truth and forget that in our beginnings we needed to learn Christian foundations and the fundamentals of our faith. Our youth and new converts must learn the same way.

Casey Treat remembers the beginning of his faith in God and is passing these teachings on in a clear and Biblical manner.

Casey Treat deals with cardinal truths of eternal life with understanding. If you build a garage, you do not need to dig deep foundations with steel and concrete; but, if you build a magnificent multistory building, you must dig deep and make your footings sure. Pastor Casey wants the new convert to dig into truth.

Pastor Casey Treat shows the joy of knowing truth. He teaches the ecstasy of the Holy Spirit and gifts of the Spirit.

This book is a guide from salvation to exaltation in praise. May it bless a multitude.

Dr. Lester Sumrall

PREFACE

In the last days, Satan will increase his work of deception throughout the earth. People are being misled into cults and religious lies as never before. The very foundations of Christianity are being challenged on every level. This book is a compilation of basic studies that show a simple picture of the foundational beliefs of Christianity.

The Bible was never meant to be a complex list of rules and traditions, so this book is not a theology treatise of each subject. Jesus said, "My Words are Spirit and life." I pray these lessons will bring His Spirit and His life into your home, family, and Christian experience. Each chapter is a simple view of a very important part of Christianity. With these basic elements you can enjoy the abundant life that Jesus has provided for all people.

1
Born Again!

Many people in this day are deceived in their belief that if they are good, law-abiding citizens they will automatically go to heaven. It's a sad thing because the truth is they won't. The Bible says you must be born again to see the kingdom of God, to be a part of the kingdom of God, to be in God's family. If they're not born again, everything written in the Bible will have no effect on them. The church is for Christian people, and Christian people are those who have been born again.

John 3:1-3 says: "There was a man of the Pharisees, named Nicodemus, a ruler of the Jews: The same came to Jesus by night, and said unto him, Rabbi, we know that thou art a teacher come from God: for no man can do these miracles that thou doest, except God be with him. Jesus answered and said unto him, Verily, verily, I say unto thee, Except a man be born again, he cannot see the kingdom of God." If you're not born again, you cannot see the kingdom of God. That's the bottom line. John 3:4-6: "Nicodemus saith unto him, How can a man be

1

born when he is old? Can he enter the second time into his mother's womb, and be born? Jesus answered, Verily, verily, I say unto thee, Except a man be born of water and of the Spirit, he cannot enter into the kingdom of God. That which is born of the flesh is flesh; and that which is born of the Spirit is spirit." Being born of the flesh is when we were born in the natural realm. Our fleshly parents caused us to be born physically. But that which is born of the Spirit is spirit. God our heavenly Father will cause us to be born spiritually. Notice where it says, "That which is born of the Spirit..." The first Spirit is capitalized. "That which is born of Spirit," capital S, "is spirit," small s. This is what Jesus literally said. When we are born of the Holy Spirit, our human spirit is what becomes born again. The body doesn't get "born" again. Jesus is talking about being born spiritually. The Holy Spirit causes my human spirit to be born a second time. My body doesn't change, my mind doesn't change, but my spirit changes.

Let's go on. John 3:7-8: "Marvel not that I said unto thee, Ye must be born again. The wind bloweth where it listeth, and thou hearest the sound thereof, but canst not tell whence it cometh, and whither it goeth: so is every one that is born of the Spirit." In other words, the wind blows where it wants to blow. You can't control it, you can't understand it, but you know it's there. You can hear the sound of it. You don't know when it's coming, and you don't know where it's going, but you know it's real. That's the way it is with being born of the

Spirit. You can't understand it, you can't control it, but you know it's real.

People often ask, "Are you a Christian or are you a born again Christian?" There are not different kinds of Christians. There's only one kind. That's the born again kind. If you're not born again, you're not a Christian. I don't care how many church rolls your name is on. If you are not born again, you are going to hell. You might say, "I give a lot of money to the poor," or "I helped build a church," or "I sat in church every Sunday," but those things don't make a bit of difference to God. If you're not born again, you will not see the kingdom of God.

When Adam sinned, all mankind was put into a position of spiritual death. That's why we have to be born again. People on this earth do not have a relationship with God in the natural. In other words, when we were out there "doing our own thing" in the world, we didn't have contact with God. We were going about our way in fellowship with the devil. But when we get born again, *then* we have fellowship *and* a relationship with the Lord.

Romans 5:12 says: "Wherefore, as by one man sin entered into the world" (Adam) "and death by sin; and so death passed upon *all men*, for that all have sinned." What "all men" literally means is all mankind, all men and women. Death came through one man and passed upon all mankind. How many of us were under that spiritual death? All of us. Is there anybody out there who doesn't need to get born again? No! It doesn't matter how good you are. It doesn't matter how many good deeds you've done. It doesn't matter how religious you are. If you are not born again, you will die and spend eternity in hell. Romans 3:23 tells us: "For all have sinned, and come short of the glory of God." What does that mean? *All* need to be born again. *All* of us need to receive this new life of God and become born again.

God so loved *all* people that He sent Jesus to save us from spiritual death. Spiritual death would be a tragedy if there was not a remedy, but He gave us salvation. He gave us a Saviour. What's His name? Jesus. The reason Jesus is our King and our Lord and the One we serve is because He saved us from that spiritual death. John 3:16 says: "For God so loved the world, that he gave his only begotten Son, that whosoever believeth in him should not perish, but have everlasting life." Whoever believes in Jesus won't die; they'll have everlasting life. Whoever believes in Jesus will be set free from the spiritual death that all mankind is subject to. We are born again. We become new people with new life, and we'll share that life for eternity with the Father. Look at Romans 6:23: "For the wages of sin is death; but the gift of God is eternal life through Jesus Christ our Lord."

What you earn in sin is death, but the gift of God is eternal life. You can't earn eternal life; you just receive it. You receive that gift from the Lord when you believe in Jesus Christ. When you have faith in Jesus, eternal life is given to you. You become a new person. You have a new life. You are born again! That's what being a Christian is all about. Ephesians 2:8-9 says: "For by grace are ye saved through faith; and that not of yourselves: it is the gift of God: Not of works, lest any man should boast."

No one can boast about what good things they've done to get saved. No one can brag about how righteous they are and how much the Lord likes them because of all they've done. All we can do is say, "Thank you Lord for your grace." All we can do is, by faith, receive what God has done and accept the gift of eternal life through Jesus Christ our Lord. It is the beginning of our relationship with God.

All of your prayers up to the point of salvation didn't do you a bit of good. I understand that's hard for some people to understand. They've been in churches for years and have prayed, burned candles, given money, and gone through religious duties. They've done dozens and dozens of works to try to have a relationship with God. Now someone comes along and shows them from the Bible it didn't mean a thing if they weren't born again. Thank God we are free from that bondage and those works. Salvation is a gift from God, and all we do is receive it by faith in Jesus Christ.

Romans 10:9-10 says: "That if thou shalt confess with thy mouth the Lord Jesus, and shalt believe in thine heart that God hath raised him from the dead, thou shalt be saved. For with the heart man believeth unto righteousness; and with the mouth confession is made unto salvation."

When you confess Jesus is Lord of your life and you believe in your heart that Jesus was raised from the dead and is alive today, you are born again. That's what makes you a Christian. When you have faith in Jesus, you have faith that He is Lord and Master of your life. When you do that, you become a new person; you have entered into a relationship with your Heavenly Father. All the work that you may have done and all the things you may have gone through up to that point did not establish a relationship with God. Your confession of faith and belief in your heart will cause God and you to become Father and son or Father and daughter. At that point in time you are a Christian; you are born again.

Becoming born again also includes repenting and turning away from all behaviors not taught in the Bible. When you are truly born again, you obey the Bible. The Bible said if you believe in Jesus then you should walk even as He walks, live like He lives.

The word "Lord" is the Greek word "kurios," and it means "the supreme authority." You're going to do what He wants you to do. Confessing Jesus as Lord and being born again means a change in your life. The change in your life does not earn your salvation. You change because you already have your salvation. You want to follow your new Lord.

When we were in the world, we followed the devil. We wanted to lie like he lies, steal like he steals, feel like he feels, and look like he looks. There's a style out there in the world. People in the world look like the one they are following, and they look worse and worse as the years go by. We want to walk like our Lord. We want to follow our God. He's Jesus. We are going to live in holiness, righteousness, and purity like He does.

The born again person is a new creature or new species of being. II Corinthians 5:17 says: "Therefore if any man be in Christ, he is a new creature: old things are passed away; behold, all things are become new." "New creature" in the Greek means "a new species of being." You are a being that never before existed. You're different than you used to be. You're the same on the outside, but you're not the same on the inside. The things that you used to enjoy you're not going to enjoy anymore because you are a new species. When you were in the world, you used to love sin, but when you came to Jesus you became a new creature. Now when you try to get back in the old life style it just doesn't feel the same anymore. You can't enjoy it because you are brand-new. You're not going to like a lot of things anymore because you are a new creature. People are going to look at you and say, "Something's different about you. You're not the same as you used to be." And you can say, "I'm a new creature in Christ Jesus. Because I have faith in Jesus, I changed." The difference is not just in your behavior and actions, but it comes from inside. When the inside of you changes, the outside begins to change also.

When we're first born again we're like young children. We must grow up by renewing our minds to the Word. A new Christian has to change the way he thinks. If we don't have a desire to change our thinking, we're not going to go very far with God. Those who want to be stubborn and believe that they've already "got it together" are not going to receive much of God's blessing. We all need to renew our minds when we come to the Lord. We all need to change the way we think. Look at Romans 12:2: "And be not conformed to this world; but be ye transformed by the renewing of your mind..."

All Christians must be transformed. They must be changed. The word "transformed" is "metamorphose," or "going through a metamorphosis" in the Greek language. That means becoming completely different. Salvation is not mental or physical; it's spiritual. Your mind is not your spirit. Your mind (along with your emotions and will) is a part of your soul. And it is up to you to change that part of you. You are responsible for what goes on in your head. You are responsible for how you feel. Feelings don't come out of the atmosphere; they come from the way you think. If you start thinking and meditating on a big problem and then start talking about it, you can get depressed real quick. What you think about controls how you feel. You are responsible to renew your mind to think positively and line up your thoughts with the Word of God.

The Bible says in Philippians 4:4: "Rejoice in the Lord alway: and again I say, Rejoice." You may think, "Well you just can't be happy all the time." That's something you can renew your mind to right now. How? You say, "I'm wrong. God said to rejoice in the Lord always, so right now I'm going to renew my mind to what God thinks. So I cast that thought out, and I make a decision to rejoice in the Lord always." That's renewing your mind. The first thing you do is say, "I'm wrong." That's the hard part because we never want to be wrong, but that's how we grow up as a Christian. Being born again is

8

the first step. As you begin to renew your mind **and change**, you will receive above and beyond what you could ask or think. As you mature, you will **get more** involved with the blessings of God.

2
Are You Filled with the Spirit?

Good *wants* to baptize us. The word "baptize" means "to immerse, submerge, fill to over-flowing." God wants to baptize us with the Holy Spirit. Who is the Holy Spirit? The Holy Spirit is God, and He is our power, strength, teacher, guide, and comforter, among other things. Acts 1:8: "But ye shall receive power, after that the Holy Ghost is come upon you: and ye shall be witnesses unto me..." John 14:26: "But the Comforter, which is the Holy Ghost, whom the Father will send in my name, he shall teach you all things, and bring all things to your remembrance, whatsoever I have said unto you." The Holy Ghost in our lives teaches us. He shows us the way. He guides us and leads us into all the truth. That's why it is so important for Christians to be baptized with the Holy Ghost.

When you became born again, you received the Holy Spirit in one sense. You were born of the Spirit. But God wants you to be baptized with the Spirit. If I had a glass and it just had an eighth of a cup of water in it, I'd say, "This glass has water in it." And you'd agree with me. If it was full of water, it would have the same thing in it, but there would be more of it. God has caused us to be born of the Spirit, but He also wants us to be filled with the Spirit. It's not a different Spirit. You received the same Spirit when you were born again. But He wants that Spirit to be overflowing. He wants there to be a release of power. He wants there to be a flow of the Spirit. "A river of living water," Jesus said, "is the Holy Ghost working in our life." He said, "If you are thirsty, come unto me and I will give you rivers of living water." John said He was talking about the Holy Ghost. God wants us to have that flow of the Holy Spirit in our lives.

The baptism with the Holy Spirit is for every Christian. Everyone can be baptized with the Holy Spirit. There are a lot of people out there teaching things like, "It's okay for some, but it's just not for me. It's okay for you, but it's not for me." If God has anything for you, I want it; and, if He has anything for me, you should want it. He's not a respecter of persons, and He's not playing games with people. If it's for one, it's for everybody. Acts 2:37-38 tells us: "Now when they heard this, they were pricked in their heart, and said unto Peter and to the rest of the apostles, Men and brethren, what shall we do? Then Peter said unto them, Repent, and be baptized every one of you in the name of Jesus Christ for the remission of sins, and ye shall receive the gift of the Holy Ghost." How many did he tell to repent? He said to everyone, "Repent, and be baptized every one ... and you shall receive the gift of the Holy Ghost." Everyone can receive the gift of the Holy Ghost. Let's go on to verse 39: "For the promise is unto you, and to your children, and to all that are afar off, even as many as the Lord our God shall call."

Now, Peter was very bold. He didn't put any limits. He said, "This is for you; this is for your children." There were over 3,000 people standing in front of him. Don't you think that if it had been for some of them and not for everyone Peter would have said, "Now, some of you are going to get it, and some of you aren't." Wouldn't he have had to say that? But he said, "This is for you and for all your children and all that are afar off." Peter boldly said that this baptism with the Holy Spirit was for every human being alive on the planet at that time. Then he said, "Even as many as the Lord our God shall call." That means everyone who comes to Jesus, who is born again, can be baptized with the Holy Spirit. Jesus said, "These signs shall follow them that believe. In my name they will speak with new tongues." The baptism of the Holy Spirit is for all believers. Sadly, I have to agree with people when they say, "Well, I just don't believe that everybody is going to be filled with the Holy Ghost," because they are right. It's just for believers. Believers will speak with new tongues. Unbelievers won't receive it.

The first evidence of being filled or baptized with the Holy Spirit is speaking with other or new tongues. Acts 2:4 says: "And they were all filled with the Holy Ghost, and began to speak with other tongues, as the Spirit gave them utterance." The scripture didn't say they were all filled with the Holy Ghost and started foaming at the mouth, rolling on the floor, and jumping up the walls. That's what a lot of people think will happen. It didn't say they were all filled with the Holy Ghost and started shaking. It didn't say they were all filled with the Holy Ghost and ran around and started hugging everybody. It didn't say they were all filled with the Holy Ghost and everybody got goose bumps and chills went up their backs. None of those things happened. All of that is religious tradition that has been passed on through people who didn't know what they were talking about. The first evidence of being filled or baptized with the Holy Spirit is speaking with other tongues.

Many years after the day of Pentecost, Peter was preaching to Cornelius' household, who were Gentiles. Acts 10:44-45 says: "While Peter yet spake these words, the Holy Ghost fell on all them which heard the word. And they of the circumcision which believed were astonished, as many as came with Peter, because that on the Gentiles also was poured out the gift of the Holy Ghost." Now how did they know that they had received the Holy Ghost? The Bible says: "For they heard them speak with tongues, and magnify God." If they hadn't heard them speak with tongues, they wouldn't have known they had received the Holy Ghost. "Oh, yes, Brother, I got it." Well, how do you know you got it? "Well, I had goose bumps all over." "Well, I foamed at the mouth." I'm not going by all that stuff. "Well, I got this warm feeling in my chest one day." I'm not going to buy that either. I'm going to go by what the

13

Bible says. I know you have received the Holy Ghost when you start speaking in tongues. That's what the apostles went by, that's what the Bible goes by, and that's what we're going to go by. Mark 16:17 says: "And these signs shall follow them that believe; In my name shall they cast out devils; they shall speak with new tongues."

Believers have evidence. They have signs that follow them. What is one of those signs? They speak with new tongues. The religious world doesn't want to do that. The religious world doesn't mind if you read the Bible as long as you don't get spiritual. The religious world doesn't mind if you sit in church as long as you don't get involved with the Holy Ghost. The first evidence of your involvement with the Holy Ghost is you begin to speak with new tongues. I think it's about time that Christians stood up and started letting the world know, "Yes, we're 'tongue talkers,' and we're glad of it. Glory to God!" I went to a church that discouraged speaking in tongues in church because it might embarrass somebody. That's ridiculous! It's a sign, a testimony, that will show the world we have the Holy Ghost.

Your mind does not understand tongues. It is a spiritual prayer. Look at I Corinthians 14:2: "For he that speaketh in an unknown tongue speaketh not unto men..." Somebody said, "Well, I don't see why you pray in tongues. I can't understand it." Just tell them, "I'm not talking to you or to any man. I'm talking to God." I Corinthians 14:2: "...For no man understandeth him; howbeit in the spirit he speaketh mysteries." The person who speaks in tongues doesn't understand it with his mind. He is speaking from his spirit, not from his head. Part of the problem most Christians have is that they want to do everything out of their heads, but God wants us to act out of our spirit. I Corinthians 14:14: "For if I pray in an unknown tongue, my spirit prayeth, but my understanding is unfruitful." When you pray in an unknown tongue, your spirit prays, but your mind doesn't understand. When you're praying in tongues, your mind is just going along for the ride. You just tell it to sit back and be quiet and you'll talk to it when you're ready. There are other times when you use your mind, but when you pray in tongues you use your spirit.

Praying in tongues is spiritual, not mental. When you're helping others receive the Holy Ghost, nine times out of ten the one problem they have is wanting to understand it, wanting to figure it out. They'll never do it. God is so big that they can't figure out how He's working. If He said to pray in tongues, just believe He knows what He is talking about. Do *you* understand how God's going to get you off this earth into heaven? No, but you believe He's going to do it; don't you? Are you worried about it? No! You just trust that He will take care of it. Just do what the Bible said, and you'll receive the blessing. I Corinthians 14:15 says: "What is it then? I will pray with the spirit, and I will pray with the understanding also..."

For us, the understanding is English. Notice he said, "I will." "I will pray with the Spirit. I will pray in English." Paul could have prayed in Greek or Hebrew or whatever other languages he knew,

and that would have been "the understanding" **for him**. Some of us may be able to speak some other language, but the understanding is what you speak out of your mind. Tongues come out of the spirit. I Corinthians 14:15: "... I will sing with the spirit, and I will sing with the understanding also."

Notice it's an act of your will. When will you pray in tongues? When you use your will and do it. I can do it right now if I want to. "Oh, Brother Treat, do you have a special anointing to do that?" No, I just said, "I will," so I did. It's an act of your will by the Holy Spirit. Luke 11:13: "If ye then, being evil, know how to give good gifts unto your children: how much more shall your heavenly Father give the Holy Spirit to them that ask him?"

If you'll ask Him for the Holy Spirit, the Father will give Him to you. If you asked for a piece of bread, He wouldn't give you a rock. If you asked for a piece of fish, He wouldn't give you a scorpion. If you ask for the Holy Spirit, He will give Him to you.

You need to pray regularly in the Holy Ghost. That builds you up. Jude 20 says: "But ye, beloved, building up yourselves on your most holy faith, praying in the Holy Ghost." It strengthens your spirit man and gives you spiritual power. It's like charging a battery. I Corinthians 14:4 says when you pray in an unknown tongue you edify yourself. You may feel spiritually weak and have had some trouble overcoming things in your life. When you pray in tongues for an hour or so every day, you'll get strong and you'll overcome those things. You build yourself up; you charge your spiritual battery.

The baptism with the Holy Spirit and praying in tongues opens a whole realm of power every Christian needs to live the powerful, overcoming life God desires all His children to have. When we generate that power by praying in tongues, it will produce certain benefits which I have listed below. When you pray in tongues you:

1) *Edify the inner man.* I Corinthians 14:4: "He that speaketh in an unknown tongue edifieth himself; but he that prophesieth edifieth the church."

2) *Receive revelation knowledge.* I Corinthians 14:2,18: "For he that speaketh in an unknown tongue speaketh not unto men, but unto God: for no man understandeth him; howbeit in the spirit he speaketh mysteries. I thank my God, I speak with tongues more than ye all."

3) *Enable yourself to turn off your mind and hear your spirit.* I Corinthians 14:14: "For if I pray in an unknown tongue, my spirit prayeth, but my understanding is unfruitful."

4) *Intercede for things.* Romans 8:26: "Likewise the Spirit also helpeth our infirmities: for we know not what we should pray for as we ought: but the Spirit itself maketh intercession for us with groanings which cannot be uttered."

5) *Pray the perfect will of God.* Romans 8:27: "And he that searcheth the hearts knoweth what is the mind of the Spirit, because he maketh intercession for the saints according to the will of God."

6) *Build yourself up in your holy faith.* Jude 20: "But ye, beloved, building up yourselves on

17

your most holy faith, praying in the Holy Ghost."

7) *Bring rest and refreshment.* Isaiah 28:11,12: "For with stammering lips and another tongue will he speak to this people. To whom he said, This is the rest wherewith ye may cause the weary to rest; and this is the refreshing: yet they would not hear."

8) *Help keep your tongue in line with the Spirit.* James 3:6,8-10: "And the tongue is a fire, a world of iniquity: so is the tongue among our members, that it defileth the whole body, and setteth on fire the course of nature; and it is set on fire of hell. But the tongue can no man tame; it is an unruly evil, full of deadly poison. Therewith bless we God, even the Father; and therewith curse we men, which are made after the similitude of God. Out of the same mouth proceedeth blessing and cursing. My brethren, these things ought not so to be."

9) *Give thanks and magnify God.* Acts 10:46 & I Corinthians 14:16,17: "For they heard them speak with tongues, and magnify God." "Else when thou shalt bless with the spirit, how shall he that occupieth the room of the unlearned say Amen at thy giving of thanks, seeing he understandeth not what thou sayest? For thou verily givest thanks well, but the other is not edified."

10) *Tongues are a sign to unbelievers.* Mark 16:17 & I Corinthians 14:22: "And these signs shall follow them that believe; In my name shall they cast out devils; they shall speak with new tongues." "Wherefore tongues are for a sign,

not to them that believe, but to them that
believe not: but prophesying serveth not for
them that believe not, but for them which
believe."

3
Commitment to the Bible

Y ou must dedicate yourself to believing and then living the Word of God. A lot of people say they are committed to the Bible and say that they believe the Bible, but their commitment consists of having the Bible sitting on the coffee table, and they look at it religiously. A true New Testament believer needs to have a commitment to *live* the Bible.

The Bible is God's will told to man so we can live the way Jesus lived and receive God's blessing. A lot of people say, "I wonder if it is God's will to heal?" All you have to do is open your Bible. I Peter 2:24 says: "Who his own self bare our sins in his own body on the tree, that we, being dead to sins, should live unto righteousness: by whose stripes ye were healed." Mark 16:18 says: "They shall lay hands on the sick and they shall recover." James 5:14-15 says: "Is any sick among you? let him call for the elders of the church; and let them pray over him, anointing him with oil in the name of the Lord: And the prayer of faith shall save the sick, and the Lord shall raise him up..." Every scripture

I've just quoted states that it is God's will to heal everybody. I don't have to question it anymore. It is God's will to heal everybody. How do I know that? Because the Bible said it. We base what we believe on the Word of God, and that is the Bible. If it's stated in the Bible, we believe it. That's the attitude we need to have. Let's look at I Thessalonians 2:13: "For this cause also thank we God without ceasing, because, when ye received the word of God which ye heard of us, ye received it not as the word of men, but as it is in truth, the word of God, which effectually worketh also in you that believe."

Paul is talking to the people in Thessalonica, and he said, "I thank God for you because when you heard the Word, when you heard my preaching and teaching, you received it as it really is, the Word of God." When God says something, it's real, it's eternal. Heaven and earth will pass away, but His Word is not going to change. Your physical health will change. Your checkbook will change. Your house will change. Your car will change. Your feelings will change. The color of your hair will change, but the Word of God won't change. Doctors' reports will change. Financial statements will change, but God never will.

When God said it, that settled it. Psalms said, "Thy word is forever settled in Heaven." When God said, "I bore their sickness and carried their disease," it was settled forever that every human being should be well. God went so far as to say, "I have exalted my Word even above my name." To find the Word of God not true would be to catch God in a lie. Do you know who the father of all liars is?

The devil. So you will never catch our Father God lying. That means you will never find any time or any place where the Word of God is not true. Now, you will find some people who don't receive the Word of God as it truly is. You can hear them say, "Well, you really never know what it means. There's so many different interpretations. You really don't know what the Bible says. It just says whatever you want it to say."

For those who do receive the Word, notice what Paul said: "It is effectually at work in you that believe." If you'll accept and commit your life to the Bible, it will begin to work in you. I Thessalonians 2:13 in the Amplified Bible says: "We also especially thank God continually for this, that when you received the message of God which you heard from us, you welcomed it not as the word of men, but as what it truly is, the word of God. Which is effectually at work in you who believe, exercising it's super human power in those who adhere to, and trust in, and rely upon it." The Word is exercising superhuman power in me because I am adhering to it, I'm living it, I'm believing it, I'm relying upon it. I put myself so far out on a limb hanging on the Word of God that if the Word ever fails I'm in trouble. I'm putting my whole trust in it. Everything I'm saying and everything I'm doing is based on the Word. If it doesn't work, I'm going under. But thank God that won't happen because the Word does work. The Word is true. The Word of God will never fail.

All Christians are to learn what the Bible says, not just a few of us, not just the clergy. II Timothy

2:15 says: "Study to shew thyself approved unto God, a workman that needeth not to be ashamed, rightly dividing the word of truth." If you don't study, you won't be approved unto God. You will be a workman that will be ashamed, and you will *wrongly* divide the Word of truth. In other words, if you want to misunderstand the Bible and say things that aren't true, then don't study it. I believe all of us want to be approved of God. All of us want to be under the blessing of God. None of us wants to be ashamed. We all want to rightly divide the Word. Read it. Meditate on it. Learn what's in the Bible. That doesn't mean that you have to be a Greek or Hebrew scholar or you have to spend hours every day with your nose buried in the book. It simply means that you apply some time in your life on a regular basis to study the Bible and find out what it says. Just listening to a message on Sunday morning is not an ample supply of the Word of God in your life.

Now, if you come to Christian Faith Center on a regular basis, you will hear a lot of Word; forty-five minutes to an hour Sunday morning, Sunday night, Wednesday night, women's advances, men's meetings, home meetings, women's bible studies, men's bible studies, seminars, and conventions, but even that's not enough. That's not going to cause you to rightly divide the Word of truth. When you go to college, if the only thing you do is show up in class, you're probably not going to make it through school. You go to class to get the basics, but then you study the books and the papers and do the research on your own. The homework is where you really get the benefits. In church we give you the basics. If you'll go out and study the Word and apply the Word and seek after the Word on your own, you'll get many more benefits and you'll really be blessed. II Timothy 3:16 says: "All scripture is given by inspiration of God..."

That literally means God breathed it into existence. Inspiration means "breathed." God breathed it, and God spoke it through men. Men wrote down the Bible by the inspiration of God. It was a divine process. It was a Godly process. It wasn't man's plan or man's idea. Man wouldn't have written some of the things in this book. They would have skipped over it and left it out, edited it. But God inspired the writers. It took forty different writers over 1600 years, starting with Moses and the Pentateuch, which is the first five books of the Bible, going on through the entire Old and New Testaments, ending up with the book of Revelation, which gives us a picture of the end time events and how we are going to be ushered up into eternity. What happens after that? He didn't say, but it's going to be good when we get there. God inspired this book to be put together. It is the work of the Spirit.

Somebody says, "Well, I just don't believe the Bible. It's just a bunch of myths. It's just a bunch of men's ideas." Myths and men's ideas don't change worlds. The Word of God has affected the world. Myths don't heal people. Myths don't set people free from depression and bondage and poverty. Many of you know what it is to be set free from depression and free from poverty because of the

Word of God.

The Bible is a different book. Nations and countries have not killed and burned and fought and gone to war over myths. But they've done it over the Word of God. We often take it for granted because most of us have 14 different translations of the Bible. I have a little one sitting in my car, four or five sitting on my desk at work, about 35 sitting in my office at home, and two or three floating somewhere. But there are people in the world praying, "God, could I have one page of a Bible?" It has to be smuggled through their police to get it to them. Then they might get killed if they get caught with it. The Bible is different. It is inspired of God. It is worth living for, and it is worth dying for.

All scripture is given by inspiration of God and is profitable. Do you want to profit? Get into the Word. Notice the things it is profitable for. II Timothy 3:16-17: "All scripture is given by inspiration of God, and is profitable for doctrine, for reproof, for correction, for instruction in righteousness: That the man of God may be perfect, thoroughly furnished unto all good works." That means perfected or fully equipped for every good work. If you get into the Word of God, it will confront you. It will challenge you. It will correct you. It will instruct you to live a righteous, holy life. It will equip you for everything that you will ever have to do in this world today. Businessmen will learn how to be successful through the Word of God. Homemakers will learn how to be successful through the Word of God. Preachers can learn how to be successful through the Word of God. (I wish more of them would learn how to preach through the Word, rather than through their seminary.) It will perfect you for every good work. Some of you businessmen have been wracking your brains, trying to figure out what to do. Start studying the Word, and the Lord will tell you what to do.

God knows how to prosper businessmen. You had better know that the Israelites, the Jewish people, know how to be blessed. Who have they been following? God. The first one who followed Him was Abraham, and he became very rich in silver and gold. Solomon came along and became the richest man the world has ever known. He had so much he didn't even bother counting the silver anymore. He had mountains of silver and gold. How did that happen? He studied the Word of God. His father David told him proverbs and lessons out of the Word. Solomon obeyed that, and God prospered him. If you will base your life on the Bible, study it and live it, you will prosper. God will show you how to have the very best of everything.

Don't believe only what you think is in the Bible. You are responsible to study it and find out what it says and then believe it. When I'm preaching in church, I don't want people agreeing with me because they think what I'm saying sounds good. I hope they have their Bibles open and are following along. Look it up in the Word and say, "That's what it says in the Word. Amen." We don't believe it just because someone said it, and we don't believe it just because we think it's in there.

There's a saying, "You know what the Bible said: Cleanliness is next to Godliness." The Bible doesn't say that, but probably nine-tenths of the world thinks it does. "If it sounds like King James English, it must be from the Bible." "Well, you know what the Bible says: God helps those who help themselves." That's not in the Bible, but they think it is. It sounds kind of spiritual. That's why certain religious sects can knock on your door and say, "Well, you know what the Bible says ..." And because people are ignorant they just sit there and say, "It does?" "Sure," they say, "Look right here." Then they hold up their own "Bible" translation, something they twisted all up by pulling out a few verses they like and leaving out the ones they didn't like. The Christian stands at the door, and he thinks he knows what the Bible says. He doesn't want to look foolish, so he says, "Why, sure enough. Look at that." They are deceived and led astray because they never took the time "to study to show themselves approved unto God." They believe what they've heard. They believe what they think is in there, but they really don't know. A lot of people are trying to get healed on what they've heard me say or what they've heard other preachers say. You can't get it based on what you heard someone else say. You've got to get it on what you heard God say. Therefore, you have to know what is in the Bible yourself.

A lot of times I ask people, "Are you born again?" "Well, of course I'm born again." "How do you know that?" "Well, one day I was driving in my car, and I felt this warm feeling come over me like oil poured over my head, and I said, 'It must have been God,' and in my heart something said, 'Yes, that's

God.' And I said, 'Hallelujah. Praise the Lord. I know I'm born again.' " Now, I hope that you're not basing your eternal life on a warm feeling. "Oh, but, Brother Treat, I know that that experience was real." I don't question that, but real experiences don't get you to heaven. Getting born again gets you to heaven. Most people can't tell you if they are born again or not. Are you born again? "Well, I sure do hope so." I do, too, but that's not going to do it. If you are born again, you can say, "Yes." "How do you know?" "Because the Bible said that if you confess with your mouth Jesus is Lord and believe in your heart that God raised Him from the dead, then you are saved. (Romans 10:9-10) And whosoever believeth that Jesus is the Christ is born of God. And whatsoever is born of God overcometh the world. Therefore, I am a world overcomer. I know I am born again because of the Word." That person is born again. The benefits of the Word come to you when you know it personally, when you get involved with it, when you know what it says, when you've acted on what it says.

I might ask someone, "Are you filled with the Holy Ghost?" "Oh, yes, Brother Treat. Glory to God. Hallelujah. I'm Pentecostal. I can run around the church and shout till my mouth foams." Yes, but are you filled with the Holy Ghost? "Doesn't that prove I am?" No. You can go to a football game and do that. The Bible said they were all filled with the Holy Ghost and began to speak in tongues. (Acts 2:4) "Well, I don't believe that part." Well, then I'd have to say you're not filled with the Holy Ghost. We're not going by your feelings or goose bumps. We're going by the Word.

Did you know that the devil can give you some experiences? The Bible says the devil comes as an angel of light. I heard of a fellow who was sick and praying for healing, but he wasn't sure if God wanted to heal him. He hoped, he wished, he prayed, but nothing happened. One morning, as he was lying in bed, it was still dark out. A bright light began to shine in his room. He opened his eyes, and he saw a white robe with sandaled feet walking across the room. Before he could lift his head, a voice said, "Yes, it is true that God heals, but not all, and God has chosen not to heal you." It disappeared before he could look up. Now that was real; I believe he saw that. I don't question the man's integrity. He truly did see that: white robe, sandaled feet, bright light. Must be Jesus. Anybody who shows up in a white robe and sandals has got to be Jesus. Right? No. I am not going to base what I know on a vision or a spirit. If it had been me, I would have said, "Get out of here, Devil, in the name of Jesus. With His stripes I was healed." But an unaware Christian, one who does not know the Word of God for himself, would be deceived. "Oh, I had a personal visitation from the Lord." He did, but from the wrong lord.

The god of this world visited that man. Years went by, and he was still sick. Finally he heard someone preaching that Jesus healed all who were sick and He desires for everyone to be well. He finally realized, "I was deceived. The devil came as an angel of light and tricked me and kept me sick all these years." The man repented, turned his faith toward God, and got healed. He could have been healed long before if he had gone by the Word and not by that vision. The benefits of the Word are received when you know it personally on particular subjects that are important to you.

Let's go through some scripture.

Salvation Romans 1:16: "I am not ashamed of the gospel of Christ: for it is the power of God unto salvation to every one that believeth; to the Jew first, and also to the Greek."

The only way you are going to get saved is to get the Word of God either through a tape, or a tract, a preacher, a TV program, a radio broadcast. Somehow you are going to have to receive the Word of God before you can get saved. God will get it to you somehow, and if you will respond to it your faith will rise up and you will get saved. That's the way to salvation—the Word of God.

Faith Romans 10:17: "So then faith cometh by hearing, and hearing by the word of God."

Without faith you cannot please God. Jesus said, "According to your faith be it unto you." Faith is the way that we receive all the blessings of God. Everything God has provided you receive by faith, but you can't get faith by praying for it. You can't get faith just by wanting it. You get faith by the Word. A lot of people say, "Oh, pray for me that my faith would be stronger." I wish I could, but it won't do any good. We could pray and lay hands on you until we rub all the hair off your head, but it still wouldn't do any good. Faith comes by hearing and hearing by the Word of God. You build your faith up when you increase your knowledge of the Word. If you are having a problem having faith for something, it is simply because the Word level in your life, in that area, is low.

Some people just can't believe that God would prosper them. It's because they haven't received enough Word about God's prosperity. Some people just can't believe that God wants them healthy. They don't have enough Word to realize the will of God concerning their health. If you get your Word level up, you will get healed. How do you do that? By reading it, by meditating on it. You do that by buying tapes and listening to them, by reading books and studying on it, by going to seminars. When the church door flies open, you fly in. Your faith level will rise up. Why? Because your Word level has risen up.

If I ever have a situation where I'm kind of shaky, I get my tapes out on that particular subject. I just pump it in there. It's like a tire. When the tire is flat, it's because it's lacking some air. How do you get it fixed? You pump the air in there. That's what is happening with many of our Christian lives. We're running around here like flat tires. We're trying to stay healthy, pay our bills, trying to give and be good Christians. We want to give, we want to be a good testimony, but we are like a flat tire. What's the problem? You've got to build your Word level up. Take every advantage you can.

Guidance Psalm 119:105: "Thy word is a lamp unto my feet, and a light unto my path."

God's Word directs and guides you. Some of you keep making wrong decisions and getting into bad situations. You need to get the Word of God in you so

31

that it can guide you and steer you clear from those problems.

Freedom John 8:31-32: "Then said Jesus to those Jews which believed on him, If ye continue in my word, then are ye my disciples indeed; And ye shall know the truth, and the truth shall make you free."

How do we become free from bondage, depression, oppression, sickness and disease? The Word of God. Abide in the Word and you'll know the truth, and the truth will make you free.

Healing Psalm 107:20: "He sent his word, and healed them, and delivered them from their destructions."

The Word of God will bring healing. He sent His Word and healed them. People who need healing need to be on an emergency program. Overdose on the Word. If a doctor says you have to show up to plug into the kidney machine or you have to show up to get your chemotherapy or you have to take two pills at a certain time every day, you do it. If you don't you might die. The Word of God has another prescription. You get the Word of God in you and study to show yourself approved unto God. The Word of God brings your faith level up. If you do it regularly, as a prescription from the doctor, you'll get well. If you will take the Word of God like you take your medicine, you'll get well. Proverbs 4:20-22 says: "My son, attend to my words; incline thine ear unto my sayings. Let them not depart from thine eyes; keep them in the midst of thine heart. For they are life unto those that find them, and health to all their flesh."

Prosperity Psalm 1:1-3: "Blessed is the man that

walketh not in the counsel of the ungodly, nor standeth in the way of sinners, nor sitteth in the seat of the scornful. But his delight is in the law [Word] of the Lord; and in his law [Word] doth he meditate day and night. And he shall be like a tree planted by the rivers of water, that bringeth forth his fruit in his season; his leaf also shall not wither; and whatsoever he doeth shall prosper."

A Christian does not associate with the ungodly. A Christian is not involved with non-Christians. This is not to say you're rude and won't talk to non-Christians but your life style is a Christian life style, and your delight must be in the Lord and His Word. That will cause you to live in God's blessing and prosper in all that you do.

Success Joshua 1:8: "This book of the law shall not depart out of thy mouth; but thou shalt meditate therein day and night, that thou mayest observe to do according to all that is written therein: for then thou shalt make thy way prosperous, and then thou shalt have good success."

A lot of people say, "Well, Brother Treat, I don't understand why I'm not succeeding." "Are you in the Word?" "Well, I come to church." "But are you studying the Word?" "Well, I don't have time for that." "Well, God doesn't have time to make you a success either."

The Word of God is not just dead letters. It is full of spirit, life, and power. Hebrews 4:12: "For the Word of God is quick, and powerful, and sharper than any two edged sword." A novel or some other book in the world is not alive; it is just knowledge. It's just material or just words. But the Word of God is alive. It's powerful. There's enough power in the Word to change your physical body. You can walk into an office quoting Shakespeare, and they might think you're poetic. But if you walk in and start quoting Jesus people get uptight. What's the difference? The Word is powerful. Walk in and say, "I learned that Jesus said, 'Except a man be born again he cannot see the kingdom of heaven. That which is born of flesh is flesh, and that which is born of the Spirit is spirit.' I found out that if you confess Jesus is Lord and believe in your heart God raised Him from the dead you'll be saved and if you don't you'll die and go to hell." You are going to have sparks flying. Why? Because Jesus, the Word, is powerful, and the devil's going to get uptight.

Just knowing the Word will produce no benefit; it must be acted on. The Bible is to be our life style. Every minute of every day of your life should be with the Word of God—when you're lying down and when you're getting up, when you're eating, when you're sleeping, when you're driving, when you're working—every minute with the Word of God. We're talking life style. *God* wants you to have a certain life style—all day, every day. Matthew 7:21-27: "Not every one that saith unto me, Lord, Lord, shall enter into the kingdom of heaven; but he that doeth the will of my Father which is in heaven. Many will say to me in that day, Lord, Lord, have we not prophesied in thy name? and in thy name have cast out devils? and in thy name done many wonderful works? And then will I profess unto them, I never knew you: depart from me, ye that work iniquity. Therefore whosoever heareth these sayings of mine, and doeth them, I will liken him unto a wise man, which built his house upon a rock: And the rain descended, and the floods came, and the winds blew, and beat upon that house; and it fell not: for it was founded upon a rock. And every one that heareth these sayings of mine, and doeth them not, shall be likened unto a foolish man, which built his house upon the sand: And the rain descended, and the floods came, and the winds blew, and beat upon that house; and it fell: and great was the fall of it." The Word of God is to be the way we live. We build our whole life on it. James 1:22-25 says: "Be ye doers of the word, and not hearers only, deceiving your own selves. For if any be a hearer of the word, and not a doer, he is like unto a man beholding his natural face in a glass: For he beholdeth himself, and goeth his way, and straightway forgetteth what manner of man he was. But whoso looketh into the perfect law of liberty, and continueth therein, he being not a forgetful hearer, but a doer of the work, this man shall be blessed in his deed."

Every person that has gone to hell in the last 2,000 years thought about getting born again because everyone that goes there had a chance to avoid it. That's a sad fact, a sad thought. Thinking about it doesn't help you. "Well I intended on it." Intentions don't help you either. If you're a wife, how often do you suppose your husband has thought about getting you some flowers? Do you really care? No. What you care about is how often he bought them. How do you suppose God feels when He looks down here and we're thinking about doing the Word but *not* doing it. What you think about is not what gets results. What you *do* is what gets results. The Word of God is not something we think about; it is something we do. James said we will be blessed in our deeds. I John 2:3: "And hereby we do know that we know him, if we keep his commandments."

How can you be certain you know the Lord? If you get goose bumps when you go to church? If you show up for every church service? No, it said you know that you know Him when you do or keep His Word. I John 2:4: "He that saith, I know him, and keepeth not his commandments, is a liar, and the truth is not in him." "Do you know the Lord?" "Oh, yes, Brother Treat. Glory to God!" "Do you pray in tongues?" "Well, I don't believe that part." "Do you lift your hands and shout, 'Hallelujah,' and praise God?" "We don't do it that way." "Do you bring your tithes and offerings to the storehouse?" "Now, just stay out of my private business." "Do you lay hands on the sick and cast out devils, intercede for the lost and for the world and for our government?" "Well, we're not into those kinds of things, Brother Treat." The Bible said if you don't do those kinds of things you're a liar.

I want you to realize how important it is to do the Word, how important it is to do what the Word of God says. If you say you know Him, you keep His Word. If you say you know Him but you don't keep His Word, then you are a liar. God said that! He can be that blunt. I John 2:5: "But whoso keepeth his word, in him verily is the love of God perfected:

hereby know we that we are in him." How do we know we're in Him? We keep His Word.

4
Baptism: Not an Option

Before Jesus went to heaven He gave His disciples some very important and specific instructions. Mark 16:15-16: "And he said unto them, Go ye into all the world, and preach the gospel to every creature. He that believeth and is baptized shall be saved; but he that believeth not shall be damned." Jesus established in His disciples' minds that baptism was not an option. It isn't something you do if you feel like it. He said, "If you believe and are baptized you will be saved." Somebody asked, "Well, if I'm not baptized but I still confess Jesus as Lord am I still saved?" If you truly confess Jesus as Lord you will get baptized because He said to do it. Anybody who says, "I confess Jesus as Lord, but I'm not going to get baptized" is not saved. They're not saved because He is not their Lord. If Jesus is your Lord you want to be baptized because you have submitted to Him.

The word baptism is the Greek word "baptizo." The Greek word means "to immerse" or "to submerge." It does not mean to sprinkle. Sprinkling became a form of baptism a couple of hundred years after Jesus died. When Jesus walked the earth, when His twelve apostles walked the earth, and when the early church began to spread after the days of Pentecost, people were baptized by being immersed in water. Matthew 28:19: "Go ye therefore, and teach all nations, baptizing them in the name of the Father, and of the Son, and of the Holy Ghost."

Again Jesus causes His apostles to understand that baptism is not an option. Baptism is a part of every Christian's life. He said to first of all teach them. Literally in the Greek it means to make a disciple out of all men. Getting people saved is not the mission of the church. The mission of the church is to make disciples. Salvation is the first step of being made a disciple. He said to baptize them in the name of the Father and the Son and the Holy Ghost after they have been made a disciple. It is God's will that you be baptized in water after you are born again. Acts 2:38: "Then Peter said unto them, Repent, and be baptized every one of you in the name of Jesus Christ for the remission of sins, and ye shall receive the gift of the Holy Ghost."

Repent doesn't mean to say you are sorry. Repent means to change your thinking. Instead of the way you used to think, make Jesus Lord. Confess Him as the Lord of your life. Change the way you think about Him and then be baptized. You are not baptized so that your sins will be remitted. You are baptized because your sins *are* remitted. You are a new creature in Christ when you repent. Then you are baptized as an outward sign of what has happened inwardly. Water will not wash away sins. Baptism will not wash away sins. There are many churches and religious groups who believe that you are a sinner and that you are bound by sin until you are baptized in water. Baptism will not wash sin out of your life. Peter said, "Be baptized for the remission of sins." We could say, "Because of the remission of sins, you shall receive the gift of the Holy Ghost." Baptism is a necessary part of the Christian experience.

The first step is being born again. Water baptism comes after the new birth. Repenting and turning to the Lord Jesus comes first. Mark 16:16 says: "He that believeth and is baptized shall be saved..." In all the verses we have read they first turned to Jesus, *then* they were baptized. Turning to the Lord Jesus is the saving aspect of it. The baptism is merely an outward expression of obedience because you are saved. *Baptism will not save you.* It is not salvation, but it is a sign that you are saved. If I made Jesus my Lord I'd immediately do what Jesus said: "Get baptized."

Babies are not yet born again and should not be baptized. We have difficulty with this because people come into the church and they have been taught to have their baby baptized as an infant. We could do it but it wouldn't be any different than sitting him in your sink and giving him a bath. There's no spiritual significance to making a baby wet. When babies are born into this world, they are born spiritually alive. Jesus said the children are of the kingdom of God. Paul said in Romans 1 that people *become* darkened. The sin nature is in their flesh, but as an infant they don't act on the sin

nature. They're just babies, and they are alive unto
God. As they grow up they begin to make choices.
Those who choose to follow God will then be born
again and their spirit will become one with the
Holy Spirit. Those who choose not to be born again
will follow after sin, after evil; their spirit then
dies. They are darkened, and they enter into sin.

It is a scientific fact that you can trace children's
lives back to when they died spiritually because
their learning abilities begin to drop off immediately. Those of you who are educators know that a
young child can learn at a much faster rate than an
adult. The reason is they are spiritually alive. You
cannot put a specific age on it. Some children will
be 6 or 7 years old. Others will be 9 or 12 years old. It
depends on several things: the child, the home, the
environment, etc. But when they reject God they
become darkened. They begin to head off in the
direction of the devil. Some of you were brought up
in church, and you were taught you were born sin-
ful, dead, and evil. It's true that your flesh was born
with the sin nature in it. You got your flesh from
your mother and your father. But where did you get
your spirit? From God. Children are born with sin-
ful natures in the flesh, but they are born alive in
their spirit. If they choose God, they'll be a new
creature in Christ. If they reject God, they will be
darkened. They must then be born again or they
will die and go to hell. It doesn't do any good to baptize babies. They are not responsible. They are not
aware. They cannot repent.

A lot of parents have hurt their children without
being aware of what they were doing. They wanted

the children to be blessed, so they'd say to their little five-year-old, "Do you believe in Jesus? Do you repent of your sins?" A little five-year-old says, "I repent of all my sins. I stole a cookie last week, and I'm sorry." So Mom or Dad say, "Okay, do you want to get baptized?" That five-year-old doesn't have the foggiest idea of what you are talking about. He's just going along with it because he wants to do whatever his parents are doing. If a parent said, "We're all going to go to church and hang upside down in the name of the Lord. Do you want to do that?" they would say, "Yes!" They are five years old and they're going to do anything mommy and daddy say.

Let the children get to the place where they can understand what's going on and make their own choice. When it comes to baptism and the New Birth, let them say, "I'm ready to commit my life to Jesus." If you force them or urge them into it when they are too young to understand, when they get to be teenagers they'll look back and say, "That wasn't anything. I didn't even know what I was doing. I don't even remember what I did. I'm only going on what Mom told me I did." If you're only saved because of what your mom told you, I have to wonder if you are saved. When I stand before the Lord I'm not going to say, "Mommy said I was saved." No! I'm going to say, "Hey, Lord, I know I made you Lord of my life. I confessed you with my mouth, and I believed in you with my heart. I am born again." Don't put your little children in a bad spot. Let them choose. Let them grow up and let them make the decision of when to make Jesus their Lord. This doesn't mean that we don't teach them and train them and love them.

Only those who have confessed Jesus as Lord should be baptized. The Bible doesn't say, "Those who signed the church roster." It doesn't say, "Those who are on the pastor's honor roll." People get baptized for a lot of reasons. Some get baptized because they think it's going to save their marriage. Some people get baptized because they think it's going to get them to heaven. Some people get baptized because they want to use that church for their wedding ceremony. There's all kinds of reasons. *But* there's only one legitimate reason to get baptized, and that is because you have made Jesus Christ your Lord and Master and Supreme Authority of your life. If you were baptized for any other reason, then you are not baptized. All you did was take a church bath, and they probably didn't even give you any soap!

In Luke 23:42-43 we have the story of Jesus on the cross between two thieves: "And he said unto Jesus, Lord, remember me when thou comest into thy kingdom. And Jesus said unto him, Verily I say unto thee, Today shalt thou be with me in paradise." That fellow didn't get baptized, and yet Jesus said, "You are going to be with me in paradise." He was saved. Why? Because he made Jesus Lord. In some denominations that guy would be lost because the guards wouldn't let him come off that cross to be baptized. I can just see him. "Hey, Centurion! Could you get a tank out here right away? I only have about 35 more minutes before I die. Could we have a baptism service here before I leave?" No, that's not what happened. That fellow couldn't be baptized yet he did go to heaven because he was saved or born again. Those of us who live after we are born again are baptized as a sign of the work that has already taken place in our heart.

Did you know that in early church days the Jews were the biggest persecutors of the Christian church? But Jews did not concern themselves with someone unless they were baptized. When someone was baptized in water, the Jewish people would actually hold a funeral and bury an empty casket and consider that person dead. They didn't do it when someone just went to church or hung around Christians but when they got baptized. They knew then because of an outward sign and they considered that person dead as far as the Jewish religion was concerned. Baptism was that powerful in the early church. A lot of people now consider it just a religious routine. But we need to understand that it is a necessary, vital part of our Christian experience.

To be baptized is to be immersed or submerged in water. Let me show this in the Bible. Philip had been preaching Christ to an Ethiopian in a chariot, going through the desert. Acts 8:35-36: "Then Philip opened his mouth, and began at the same scripture, and preached unto him Jesus. And as they went on their way, they came unto a certain water: and the eunuch said, See, here is water; what doth hinder me to be baptized?" Notice it's apparent that Philip taught this man that being baptized was part of being a Christian. As soon as he saw water the Ethiopian said, "Hey, can I get baptized?

What's stopping me?" Philip instructed him that it was a vital and necessary part of his Christian life. Verse 37 says: "And Philip said, If thou believest with all thine heart, thou mayest..." What was the prerequisite to baptism? If you believe with all your heart.

When you were baptized, did you believe Jesus was Lord? If you did, you followed New Testament order and you have fulfilled the stipulations of the New Testament. If you didn't, you really weren't baptized. If you didn't know, it's obvious you couldn't believe. They tell me I was baptized when I was a baby. I have to say they tell me because I don't remember. I assume they are telling me the truth, but as a child I didn't believe that Jesus was Lord. I believed in bottles and clean diapers. That's all I was interested in. Babies don't believe in Jesus. If you had a religious experience, fine. If you went to church, fine. If you were sprinkled as a baby, fine. Your parents did that because they loved you. They thought that was right. The church thought that was right. Everything was good about it, but the fact is it had nothing to do with the Bible or God. It's good, beautiful, nice, kind, sweet, but it's not Bible. We want to do what the Bible says. Acts 8:37: "...And he answered and said, I believe that Jesus Christ is the son of God."

Right there! That makes you a candidate for baptism. Do you believe that Jesus Christ is the Son of God? Okay, then you are ready to be baptized. Acts 8:38-39 goes on to say: "And he commanded the chariot to stand still: and they went down both into the water, both Philip and the eunuch; and he baptized him. And when they were come up out of the water, the Spirit of the Lord caught away Philip, that the eunuch saw him no more." Notice how Philip baptized him. He stopped the chariot, went down into the water and came out of the water. That doesn't sound like sprinkling to me. If I was going to sprinkle him I'd say, "We went over to the shore of the water. I grabbed a handful of water and dripped it on his head." The Bible said they both went down into the water and they both came up out of the water. To some people, their tradition is more important than the Bible. Not to me! My Bible is more important than any tradition. Traditions come and go, but the Bible always stays.

In the New Testament people were immersed when they were water baptized. We need to be scriptural, not traditional. Water baptism is an outward sign of what has happened inwardly when we are born again. Romans 6:3-5 says: "Know ye not, that so many of us as were baptized into Jesus Christ were baptized into his death? Therefore we are buried with him by baptism into death: that like as Christ was raised up from the dead by the glory of the Father, even so we also should walk in newness of life. For if we have been planted together in the likeness of his death, we shall be also in the likeness of his resurrection." Jesus died, was buried, and resurrected in newness of life. He said you were baptized into His death and if you died with Him you were also resurrected with Him. He's talking about what took place in the spirit world. When we made Jesus Lord we were crucified with Him, buried with Him, raised up with Him in newness of life. So when you are water baptized you confess Jesus as Lord, signifying you are crucified with Christ. You give up your old life. You are dead to the world. You are dead to what you used to know and what you used to have. What do you do with dead folks? Bury them. We put you down under the water as a symbol of your being buried. The old man is dead and gone. I know the old man tries to hang around, but don't let him. The old man will pull you back into the world if you let him. Bury that old person.

Baptism symbolizes a new creature, a new person, a new man, a new woman in Jesus Christ. It is saying, "I am crucified with Christ. I am raised up with Christ as a new person." You cannot get that same meaning out of sprinkling or out of any other form of baptism. Immersion and submersion is a symbol of being dead, buried, and resurrected with Christ. That's why we are baptized as an outward sign of what has happened inwardly when we were born again.

5
Communion

Communion is to remind us of Jesus' provisions at the cross. Communion which is also called the Eucharist, the Lord's Supper, the Lord's Table, is when we take bread and juice together in remembrance of Jesus' provisions at the cross. Paul teaches about it in I Corinthians 11:23-26: "For I have received of the Lord that which also I delivered unto you, That the Lord Jesus the same night in which he was betrayed took bread: And when he had given thanks, he brake it, and said, Take, eat: this is my body, which is broken for you: this do in remembrance of me. After the same manner also he took the cup, when he had supped, saying, This cup is the new testament in my blood: this do ye, as oft as ye drink it, in remembrance of me. For as often as ye eat this bread, and drink this cup, ye do shew the Lord's death till he come." Paul quotes what Jesus said in Matthew 26 when He was taking the Last Supper. He was establishing what we now call communion or the Lord's Supper. The Old Testament Passover was a type or a symbol of what Jesus was to do on the cross. In Exodus 12:3-14 you'll read about how the Jews were in captivity to Egypt and the Lord through Moses told them to take a lamb and roast it. Then they were to take the blood of the lamb and put it on the doorpost and on the lintel. In other words, they formed the sign of the cross on their door with the blood of that lamb. They took the lamb and ate it. They were to have their shoes on, their staff in their hand, and their coat ready to go. They were ready to leave Egypt and enter into their deliverance. The blood of the lamb in the Passover signified the blood of Jesus. The lamb itself signified Jesus, who is the Lamb of God.

Remember in John 1:29: "The next day John (John the Baptist) seeth Jesus coming unto him, and saith, Behold the Lamb of God, which taketh away the sin of the world." That lamb in the Old Testament Passover feast was a type or a symbol of Jesus and what He was going to do in the New Testament. His blood cleansed us from sin and His body brought healing to us. When we look at the New Testament act of communion, we are remembering what Jesus' blood and body has done. The Jews took the blood and put it on their door and took the lamb and ate it. They realized what God was doing for them, and they were looking to their Deliverer, their Messiah which was to come. We take communion and look back at what has already come.

The Old Testament Passover was a symbol of what Jesus was going to do on the cross. The Passover was the foundation for communion. The last Passover celebration was the first communion celebration. The Last Supper which we read about in John 13, where Jesus washed people's feet and they took the wine and bread, was the last Passover. The Jews continue to celebrate Passover, but there is no reason for it. Why look ahead to something that has already happened? They continue to take the Passover because they missed the Messiah. They rejected the real Lamb of God. They crucified the Lamb of God, so they continue to take the Passover, waiting for the real one to come.

We don't take Passover any more; we take communion. We don't do it just once a year like the original Jewish ceremony because the Bible says, "As oft as ye eat and drink it." God left it up to us. You can take it every day if you want to. You don't have to take communion only when you come to church. Nowhere in the Bible does it say that the pastor or the priest has to serve communion. Anytime you take bread and juice in remembrance of the Lord Jesus Christ, with honor and respect and examining yourself to Him, you can take communion. You can take it by yourself. You can take it with your family.

In fact, it would be good to do it with your family. You need to teach your children and start living the New Testament in your home because a lot of your kids think communion is only for church. It's the only place they've ever seen it done. A lot of them think that you're only supposed to sing and dance and lift your hands at church because they don't see you doing those things at home.

You can take communion whenever you want. Don't make it a light thing. That's a blight on the name of the Lord. God looks very hard at those kinds of things; but, if you are sincere before the Lord and you want to remember the death of the Lord Jesus and proclaim His coming, examine yourself, and you can take communion anywhere you want to. Pastor or no pastor, it's up to you. You're a Christian, a child of God. The Spirit of God is living in you.

We need to renew our minds to the fact that we don't go through religious ceremonies at church. This is our life. This is our life style. Sure we do it at church, but what about at home?

Jesus started the act of taking communion at the Last Supper. Matthew 26:17: "Now the first day of the feast of unleavened bread the disciples came to Jesus, saying unto him, Where wilt thou that we prepare for thee to eat the Passover?" Matthew 26:26-28: "And as they were eating, Jesus took bread, and blessed it, and brake it, and gave it to the disciples, and said, Take, eat; this is my body. And he took the cup, and gave thanks, and gave it to them, saying, Drink ye all of it; For this is my blood of the new testament, which is shed for many for the remission of sins." Here He instituted communion or the Lord's Supper. He took the bread and He took the cup. He broke the bread and said, "This is my body." He drank the cup and said, "This is my blood." There are different churches which teach that when you receive communion the juice literally becomes the blood of Jesus Christ and when you receive the bread it literally becomes the body of the Lord Jesus Christ. In this day of the church or this age of grace, physical items are not what sustain the church. The Spirit and the faith we have in the things of God makes the difference. Even if it was the physical, literal blood of Jesus, it wouldn't do a thing for you.

Jesus said, "I am the vine." Did that mean He was a bush? He said, "I am the door." Does that mean His belly button is a door knob? What is He trying to say? He's trying to show us the spiritual significance. When we get hung up on these physical things, we miss the whole idea of the spiritual significance of it. Jesus was teaching us that if we will exercise faith in what He has done when we partake of this juice and when we eat of this bread, then by His Spirit the cleansing power of His blood will operate in us; the healing power of His body will flow through us. Communion is a spiritual action. It's not the juice that does anything. It's not the bread that does anything. It is the faith that you and I have in the body and blood of the Lord Jesus Christ. That's what makes a difference.

When we take communion, we remember the Lord's death. We proclaim our faith that He is coming again, and we receive healing, strength, and long life. We must take communion seriously and take it only when we are clean or pure before the Lord. I Corinthians 11:27-29: "Wherefore whosoever shall eat this bread, and drink this cup of the Lord, unworthily, shall be guilty of the body and blood of the Lord. But let a man examine himself, and so let him eat of that bread, and drink of that cup. For he that eateth and drinketh unworthily, eateth and drinketh damnation to himself, not discerning the Lord's body."

God doesn't want you to play games with Him. He said, "When you are involved with me, you must be real." You must examine yourself and make sure you're right. Don't come in here living in adultery and then say, "I'm going to receive the body and blood of Jesus." You are still saved. He still loves you and wants to help you, but don't play around with Him. This isn't a light thing. This isn't a joke. This is the Word of God.

I don't think a lot of people have understood that. When God says, "Pray in the Spirit," that means pray in the Spirit now. When God says, "Examine yourself and see that you are worthy," I am going to look at what I can change. A lot of people still take communion when they are bitter, mad, have a bad attitude, and lying. They leave church, cuss their wife out and kick their kids. He said, "Examine yourself. Discern the Lord's body." Don't take this lightly. What are you really doing? Is this reality to you, or is this just another religious game you are floating through? I Corinthians 11:30: "For this cause many are weak and sickly among you, and many sleep." Sleep means they die young. Thank God we can turn it around and we can judge ourselves. We don't have to be weak and sickly and die young. We can be strong and healthy and live long. It comes when we examine ourselves when we partake of communion.

Some people would ask, "Why do we use juice and not wine? I thought the Bible said they used wine." In the New Testament, wine is used both sig- nifying fruit juice and alcoholic beverages. A lot of times you don't really know which one they are talking about. We have an option today in that there are enough beverages available to us we don't have to use wine. Back then, they were very limited in what they had available to them. There was no refrigeration. They had conditions they couldn't do too much about. Today we can do something about it. Wine is the greatest killer of people in the United States today. Alcohol is destroying people's lives. I certainly don't want to start pouring it in church. You say, "Oh Brother Treat, just a little tiny bit doesn't make that much difference, does it?" For some, if they got the taste on their tongue they would leave church and head for the bar. The devil is pouring enough alcohol. There is no sense in us joining him.

Communion is not a ritual or a tradition. It is not to be taken lightly. God commanded us to do it for a specific reason. If we will take heed to that and use communion as God intended it, we will find it has a powerful impact on our lives.

6
Healing: Is It for All?

Men and women were created by God to live in divine life and health. Sickness was not a part of God's plan. Genesis 1:26-31: "And God said, Let us make man in our image, after our likeness: and let them have dominion over the fish of the sea, and over the fowl of the air, and over the cattle, and over all the earth, and over every creeping thing that creepeth upon the earth. So God created man in his own image, in the image of God created he him; male and female created he them. And God blessed them, and God said unto them, Be fruitful and multiply, and replenish the earth, and subdue it: and have dominion over the fish of the sea, and over the fowl of the air, and over every living thing that moveth upon the earth. And God said, Behold, I have given you every herb bearing seed, which is upon the face of all the earth, and every tree, in the which is the fruit of a tree yielding seed; to you it shall be for meat. And to every beast of the earth and to every fowl of the air, and to every thing that creepeth upon the earth, wherein there is life, I have given every green herb for meat: and it was so. And God saw every thing that he had made, and, behold, it was very good. And the evening and the morning were the sixth day." Notice there was no mention of sickness or disease, no mention of death, simply God and man created in His image, and it was very good. Genesis 2:7: "And the Lord God formed man of the dust of the ground, and breathed into his nostrils the breath of life; and man became a living soul." If man had continued in the state God created him, he never would have died. He would have lived on this earth in fellowship with God as a living soul with the breath of life and never tasted death. This whole planet would have been like the garden of Eden. Man would not have struggled with sin or sickness or disease.

In Genesis Chapter 3 we see a third party introduced to the relationship between God and man. That, of course, is the devil. At that point we see death and sickness or disease introduced, but in God's original plan sickness or disease had no part. Death had no part. God created man and woman to live in divine life. Man didn't need healing because there was no sickness in God's presence. He didn't need deliverance because there was nothing to be delivered from. God originally established man to live in life and health all of his days on the earth.

Sickness came into the world as a result of sin and death that Satan brought. The serpent beguiled Eve. Eve gave to her husband. He ate the fruit, and they both died spiritually. Genesis 3:16 says: "Unto the woman he said, I will greatly multiply thy sorrow and thy conception; in sorrow thou shalt bring forth children; and thy desire shall be to thy husband, and he shall rule over thee." Women do not have to go through suffering and torment in childbirth. There's going to be some discomfort because in travail, in the giving of birth, there is discomfort, but you don't have to go through pain and anguish and torment. In the New Testament, it said that you have been delivered. You have been spared in childbearing *if* your faith is toward the Lord. Many women today are finding out God has delivered them from the curse that Satan brought upon the earth. They're finding out they don't have to go through the suffering in childbirth that many thought was normal. Genesis 3:17-19: "And unto Adam he said, Because thou hast hearkened unto the voice of thy wife, and hast eaten of the tree, of which I commanded thee, saying, Thou shalt not eat of it: cursed is the ground for thy sake; in sorrow shalt thou eat of it all the days of thy life; Thorns also and thistles shall it bring forth to thee; and thou shalt eat the herb of the field; In the sweat of thy face shalt thou eat bread, till thou return into the ground; for out of it wast thou taken: for dust thou art, and unto dust shalt thou return."

Previously God said, "When you eat of the fruit of the tree, you will die." Spiritual death came into Adam, and his body began to decay. That's what God was saying: "From the dust you came and from the dust you will return." That decaying process is aging, and it also carries with it sickness and disease. In the redemption at the cross, Jesus did not deliver us from aging because our bodies are not yet saved. The Bible said in Romans 8 that we are waiting for the redemption of the body. There will be a day when you won't get any older. You'll have a spiritual body, a glorified body, and you'll live that way for eternity. You will never age another second.

Although we still age, through the redemption of the cross and through the provisions of Jesus we don't have to have sickness and disease. Satan brought that upon this planet. If you will look at God's plan in the garden of Eden, you will see man and woman in life without death, sickness, or disease. If you will look at God's plan after Satan has been cast into the pit, you will see man and woman living in the presence of God without sickness or disease or death. God's plan at the beginning is the same as God's plan at the end. Everything in between is what Satan has brought.

Do you believe it is God's will for us to be sick when we get to heaven? Of course not. If it's not His will for us to be sick in heaven then it can't be His will for us when we are down here. God's not schizophrenic. He doesn't change His mind like we do. Some people think that God's like us. You say, "I'll have a hamburger. Wait a minute! I'll have a steak. I changed my mind." No, God doesn't do that. When He says something, that's it. What He says will stay for eternity. His plan at the beginning was for you to be alive, well, and strong on the earth, to have dominion and to subdue it. His plan at the end is for you to be alive, well, and strong on the earth, to have dominion and subdue it. He never changed. Satan introduced spiritual death, and Satan introduced sickness and physical death. It never was a part of God's plan.

As long as we are in this world we will have to resist the god of this world and his sin and sickness. II Corinthians 4:4: "In whom the god of this world hath blinded the minds of them which believe not, lest the light of the glorious gospel of Christ, who is the image of God, should shine unto them." Satan is still the god of this world. In Ephesians he is called the prince of the power of the air. In Peter he is called our adversary who walketh about as a roaring lion seeking whom he may devour. Even though you are saved, you haven't lost your enemy. In fact, when you got saved your enemy got more hostile. The god of this world wants to destroy us. This one verse actually explains the whole thing clearly. John 10:10: "The thief cometh not, but for to steal, and to kill, and to destroy: I am come that they might have life, and that they might have it more abundantly."

Jesus made it so clear. The devil is a thief. He comes to kill and steal and destroy, but Jesus comes to give life and life more abundantly. If you just consider every situation and every circumstance and then look to that verse, it will answer just about every question you ever have. When a circumstance comes up, all you have to do is ask yourself, "Is this killing, stealing, or destroying, or is this bringing life and life more abundant to me?" If it's killing, stealing, or destroying, you know it is the devil. You don't accept it. You refuse to let it happen in your life. You don't have to let the devil come in and run you over. You just say, "No, I'm not going to go for it. I refuse to be that way." If it's life and life more abundant, you say, "Come on in, Lord. Give it all to me." So many people have a hard time understanding. They say, "Well, I didn't know if it was of the Lord or not." If it's life and life more abundant, it's the Lord. "Well, I thought God gave you that cancer." Is that killing, stealing, and destroying or abundant life? Which one is it? Stealing, killing, and destroying. So that couldn't be Jesus. That has to be the thief.

Have you ever gone to the hospital and found all the folks rejoicing over all the abundant life they've received? No, they're getting their health robbed. Their body is being destroyed, and the devil is trying to kill them. The thief comes to do that. This is so easy to figure out. If it's killing, stealing, or destroying, it's the devil. You don't have to think. You don't have to wonder. When the devil tries to put those things on me, I know it's the devil trying to destroy my joy and destroy my life, so I just resist it. I refuse it.

If a car comes by and kills a little boy, can we stand up and say the Lord took him home? Not unless we are serving the wrong lord, because that is killing, stealing, and destroying. The thief is the one who did that. Now, thank God that little boy goes to heaven, but he didn't have to go so soon. The thief came to steal him. That verse right there sums up and gives a clear picture of God's plan and the devil's plan. God has designed men and women to live in health all the time. It's His will. That's how God created you. The devil is not in agreement with that.

Jesus was sent by the Father to undo what Satan had done, and that includes overcoming sickness and disease. In Genesis 3, Satan came and brought spiritual death. Jesus came to undo that by bringing spiritual life. Satan caused their bodies to decay and die. Jesus came to undo that. When you make Jesus your Lord, you will eventually have a glorified body, a spiritual body that decays no more and will live forever. When Satan came in he brought sickness and disease. Jesus bore that sickness and disease so you no longer have to bear it in your own body. I John 3:8 says: "He that committeth sin is of the devil; for the devil sinneth from the beginning. For this purpose the Son of God was manifested, that he might destroy the works of the devil." Jesus came to destroy what Satan is doing. When we put our faith in Jesus, we can stop that killing. We can stop that sickness and disease. We can stop that destruction. Look at Acts 10:38: "How God anointed Jesus of Nazareth with the Holy Ghost and with power; who went about doing good, and healing all that were oppressed of the devil; for God was with him."

Why would God anoint Jesus to heal people if God made them sick? Have you ever heard that the Lord is trying to teach you something by making you sick? "The Lord is trying to humble you and the Lord has allowed this." If you just read the Bible for five minutes, you will find out that is a lie. The Bible said, "God anointed Jesus, who went about doing good, healing all that were oppressed of the devil, for God was with him." God was with Jesus, setting people free from what the devil had done. What had he done? Stolen, killed and destroyed. Jesus came along to undo what Satan was doing.

Remember in Luke 13 there was a little woman who had been bent over for 18 long years. She had been sick. Jesus said, "Woman thou art loosed from thine infirmities." The Pharisees and the religious folks were saying, "Well, you shouldn't be healing people on the Sabbath day." Jesus said, "Ought not this woman whom Satan hath bound be loosed from her infirmity?" Satan is the author of sickness and disease. It never was God's plan. Jesus came to set us free from what the devil tries to bring upon us. The devil never does the works of God, and God never does the works of the devil. Some Christians say, "Well, I know that the devil causes sickness, but sometimes I know that God does." Does God sin sometimes? Then God doesn't do the work of the devil sometimes. Satan is always out to kill, steal, and destroy, but God is always out to bring life and life more abundantly. He never changes. That is always His plan. That is always His will. Isaiah 53:4-5: "Surely he hath borne our griefs, and carried our sorrows: yet we did esteem him stricken, smitten of God, and afflicted. But he was wounded for our transgressions, he was bruised for our iniquities: the chastisement of our peace was upon him; and with his stripes we are healed."

Why are we healed? Because when Jesus was bruised He bore our pain and carried our sickness. During that time on the cross, the beating and the crucifying of His flesh was also the deliverance of our flesh. Jesus died so we could live. Jesus bore sickness so we could bear health. Jesus went to hell so we could go to heaven. Jesus defeated Satan so we would have fellowship with God. Everything

Jesus did at the cross was so you could have the life that God had planned for you from the beginning. To say that God wants you to be sick is to say that what Jesus did was not enough. I don't want to get caught pointing my bony finger at God saying, "God, what you did at the cross of Calvary wasn't good enough." I want to be saying, "Yes, Lord, you did it all." Jesus bore it all. Jesus provided it all. I simply receive it and thank Him for it in His mighty name. I'm telling you, it was enough. Matthew 8:16-17 says: "When the even was come, they brought unto him many that were possessed with devils: and he cast out the spirits with his word, and healed all that were sick: That it might be fulfilled which was spoken by Esaias the prophet, saying, Himself took our infirmities, and bare our sicknesses."

This is a New Testament quotation of what we read in the Old Testament. Notice this time he used the word "sicknesses" because that is in the original Hebrew. Jesus bore my sicknesses so I don't have to be sick. Remember, the god of this world will come and lie. He'll come to kill, steal, and destroy, and he'll try and get you to bear the sicknesses yourself. All you've got to do is say, "No, Jesus already undid what you have done, and I refuse to bear what Jesus already bore for me." Look at I Peter 2:24: "Who his own self bare our sins in his own body on the tree, that we, being dead to sins, should live unto righteousness: by whose stripes ye were healed." At the same time He bore your sins on the tree, He also bore your sickness. Since you are alive unto righteousness and don't have to be in sin, you are also alive unto healing and don't have to be in sickness. Notice it said ye *were* healed. It was taken care of at the cross. That's a past tense fact. He's not going to heal you "Some day." He already took care of it at the cross.

What if I went to the bank and put $500 in your checking account. The next day you came to me and said, "Oh, Brother Treat, I'm so poor. I'm so broke. I just don't know what I am going to do." I'd say, "Look, yesterday I put $500 in your checking account." Then the next day you come back and say, "Oh, I'm so poor. I'm so broke." I'd say, "Didn't you draw out what I put in the account?" You'd say, "Oh no, I didn't really think that was for me. I just wasn't sure if it would work or not. I'm just so broke and just so poor." I'd say, "Look, Brother, your needs were met. Your financial need was taken care of." What does that mean? It's already done. The money's in the bank. Just go write a check. That's the way healing is. Healing is already provided. It's already here. Just write your check of faith. Sign "In the name of Jesus" at the bottom, and it will be yours. He's already provided it. "With His stripes ye were healed."

Salvation includes healing, and it is for *everyone.* The salvation of your spirit and the healing of your body took place at the same time. John 3:16 says: "For God so loved the world, that he gave his only begotten Son, that whosoever believeth in him should not perish, but have everlasting life." And Acts 2:21 says: "And it shall come to pass, that whosoever shall call on the name of the Lord shall be saved." The word "saved" doesn't just mean you'll go to heaven. It also means to be healed. When you are saved, you have also received healing. Now you might not use it, but it's there. It's a package deal. He said, "Whosoever calls on the name of the Lord will be saved." He gave you eternal life, healing, and prosperity. Take everything. Be a hog! God doesn't mind. God has said, "Here it is. Whosoever calls on my name shall be healed. It's for 'whosoever.' All you have to do is accept it, receive it, take it. It's yours." Luke 6:19 says: "And the whole multitude sought to touch him: for there went virtue out of him, and healed them all." They sought to touch Him because power was coming out and it healed them all. It's the same power today. It's the same Jesus today. We have the same provision today.

Salvation is translated into the Greek words "sozo" or "soteria." It means to deliver, to heal, to save, to rescue. All can have eternal life and all can be healed. If you fit into "all," it's for you. God didn't devise a plan to save you from hell and then let you suffer hell on earth. No! God's plan is to save you now and to also save you from hell.

God provided many ways to receive healing. There are at least seven and probably a few others. Let's look at Mark 11:24: "Therefore I say unto you, What things soever ye desire, when ye pray, believe that ye receive them, and ye shall have them."

That's one way to receive healing. By praying and believing that you have received. Healing is a desire of your heart. If you need healing and you pray believing that you received it, you shall have it.

It's almost like God knew that not everybody could receive in the same way so He provided many ways. James 5:14-15 tells us another way you can be healed: "Is any sick among you? Let him call for the elders of the church; and let them pray over him, anointing him with oil in the name of the Lord: And the prayer of faith shall save the sick, and the Lord shall raise him up; and if he have committed sins, they shall be forgiven him." If you just don't want to pray and believe on your own, you can call on the elders. They will anoint you with oil and pray the prayer of faith. The Lord will raise you up, and you'll be healed.

Once when Jesus walked on the earth He spit in the ground, made some clay, and slapped it in someone's eyes. That's a way that somebody got healed. I don't think we should start the association of spit mud makers but that was one way somebody got healed. Once in the Old Testament they said, "Go dip in the river seven times." The person got healed after dipping in the river. There are a number of different ways and methods God uses. Healing is for all, and God's doing everything He can to get it to all of us. Mark 16:17-18 says: "And these signs shall follow them that believe; In my name shall they cast out devils; they shall speak with new tongues; They shall take up serpents; and if they drink any deadly thing, it shall not hurt them; they shall lay hands on the sick, and they shall recover." There are no ifs, ands, or buts in that verse. Just lay hands on the sick and they'll recover. I just like to do all of them: anoint with oil, pray the prayer of faith, and lay on the hands.

The world is so full of sickness. There are doctor's offices and hospitals filled up with people who are getting sicker and sicker. But thank God the church is getting well. The world is finding out that we have some things they don't. They're finding out they don't have to go through cancer and leukemia and diabetes. Jesus has provided healing. Acts 19:11-12 says: "And God wrought special miracles by the hands of Paul: So that from his body were brought unto the sick handkerchiefs or aprons, and the diseases departed from them, and the evil spirits went out of them."

There's another way you can be healed. Have someone who is anointed with the Holy Spirit lay hands on a cloth or an apron or a towel, any type of cloth. It doesn't work with wood or metal, but any type of cloth. That anointing to heal will go into that cloth. Then go lay it on the sick person, and they will get healed. We've seen it happen. People have brought up cloths while we've been praying for the sick, and we just prayed over that cloth. They've laid it on the sick person, and that person got healed. That anointing is a force. It is a spiritual power that can be transferred just like when people touched Jesus' robe. What happened? That power flowed into them, and they were healed. The same thing happens when you lay hands on people. You are transferring that healing power into their bodies. You can put it in the cloth, take it to them and they'll be healed. Matthew 18:19-20: "Again I say unto you, That if two of you shall agree on earth as touching anything that they shall ask, it shall be done for them of my Father which is in heaven. For where two or three are gathered together in my name, there am I in the midst of them."

The prayer of agreement is another way to be healed. I Corinthians 11 teaches us you can be healed when you take communion. The Bible teaches that you can worship and praise God and get healed in the midst of that praise and worship. God has provided innumerable ways for us to receive our healing. Don't limit God. I believe that God is doing everything He can to get us healed. Why? Because it has always been God's plan for people to be healthy, whole, and strong.

7
Praise and Worship God's Way

There is a great deal of tradition around the area of praise and worship. In some churches the only reason you know it is a worship service is because that's what it says at the top of the program. They'll sing a couple of hymns, say a couple of prayers, and have a little 15- or 20-minute sermonette. Then they'll close with the benediction and call that a worship service. In that service I am sure there are things that could be called worship, but we don't want to just go by what the church has always done or what we have always seen. We want to go by what the Bible says. So I'm going to take what I believe about praise and worship right out of the scriptures, take it right out of the Word.

When you find something in the scriptures that doesn't line up with the way you have been acting, do you decide to make a change in yourself? Or do you try to change the scriptures? When we read the Bible, we should find out what God says and then line ourselves up with the Word, not the other way around. If you'll get lined up with God, you will have greater success than if you try and get God lined up with you. We can't change God. He's been around a lot longer than we have. But we can change ourselves to obey Him and to follow Him.

You say, "Yeah, but, Brother Treat, we never did it that way before." Well, praise God you have a chance to renew your mind. Do you know what they say the seven last words of the church are going to be? "We never did it that way before." Just think about this. Back in the 1700's, 1800's, and early part of the 1900's, if you had a sickness a doctor might reach into a jar and pull out a leech. That leech was put on your arm to suck for awhile. Hopefully that would heal you. Aren't you glad they don't do that today? Aren't you glad the doctor doesn't say, "Look, man, I've been hanging leeches on people for 20 years, and I ain't going to change." I'm glad they renewed their minds to leeches. They found out that wasn't the best way to get people healed. They have gained other medicines, operations, surgeries, and equipment to help people to be well. They have learned better ways of doing things.

You may have some thinking about praise and worship. You may have some ideas about the way it should be and the way that you like it. Let's be open and not get caught in a rut of tradition. Let's be open so we can progress and move on, so we can obey the scriptures to the very highest degree. Let's follow God. Ephesians 5:18-20 says: "And be not drunk with wine, wherein is excess; but be filled with the Spirit; Speaking to yourselves in psalms and hymns and spiritual songs, singing and making melody in your heart to the Lord; Giving thanks always for all things unto God and the Father in the name of our Lord Jesus Christ."

Here we see a New Testament principle of praising, singing, and singing psalms which is from the book of Psalms in the Old Testament. Singing hymns, which are songs written by men concerning spiritual things, and spiritual songs, which we would call choruses, that is a part of New Testament life. In Matthew 12 it says if you have it in your heart, then it has to come out of your mouth. Making melody in your heart to the Lord, praise and worship, singing to the Lord, should be a part of your everyday life. I Timothy 2:8: "I will therefore, that men pray everywhere, lifting up holy hands, without wrath and doubting."

I want you to see that this is a New Testament scripture. It is a New Testament principle that we lift up our hands in prayer, and of course prayer is a part of praise and worship. A lot of people say, "Well, I don't feel good lifting up my hands." God didn't ask you how you felt about it. "Well, Brother Treat, I'm kind of nervous about that." Well, so was I, but you'll get over it. You were kind of nervous about your first date, but you got over that one. Isn't that right? You were nervous about your first kiss, but you got over that one, too. You've been nervous about a lot of things, but you did it. You worked through that fear. You overcame that nervousness.

You see, the flesh will always rebel against the things of God. The flesh is nervous about praying in tongues, but we do it anyway. The flesh is nervous about submitting to the Lord Jesus Christ, but we

71

do it anyway. The flesh does not like to praise and worship God like the Bible says, but we will do it anyway if we are spiritually minded and not fleshly minded. If you want to be controlled by the devil, then do the things your flesh likes. But if you want to be controlled by God, then do the things the Bible says. It is that simple. You either make the decision to obey the Lord or you don't.

Paul said, "It is my will that men pray everywhere lifting up holy hands." That means you should be able to lift your hands anywhere. I might be walking around a shopping mall and see some friend of mine and just praise God right there. Hallelujah! Glory to God! "Oh, Brother Treat, that's just weird." Yes, but it's what the Bible said. If you want to call the Bible weird, that's fine with me, but I'm going to do what the Bible says. "Well, I never would act that way." You're never going to obey the Bible then. Isn't that terrible? It's our carnal, "seeking to please others," "seeking to be accepted by the world" attitude. That's really the only thing that stops us from obeying the Word. We're so concerned with what the world thinks. What we need is to get concerned about what God thinks. When I lift my hands in the air praising God, I don't care what you think, because I know God likes it. I care about you, I love you, but God holds higher priority.

Music and praise brings the anointing of the Holy Spirit and spiritual power. Satan knows these things because he's used them for evil, and the church has been unaware. We've avoided many of the tools and opportunities which God has given to us concerning praise and music. If we will take heed to what the scriptures say concerning music, we will find the power and a release of the Holy Spirit that is far greater than we have known before. In the world, Satan knows if he can get you involved with certain kinds of music he can get you involved with evil spirits. In rock and roll concerts, young people come forward and give their souls to Satan. They have altar calls at rock and roll concerts to commit their lives to the devil. They have healing services at rock and roll concerts saying that Satan will heal them if they come down to the front. They have sacrifices, blood sacrifices of live animals. They will bite heads off of bats, birds, cats, and dogs, just bite them off with their own teeth. They sprinkle blood all over and offer it to the devil. Now it sounds horrid, but a lot of our kids are involved with it. The devil knows that music is a vehicle for spiritual power, and he'll use it for evil. Thank God we can use it for good. If we'll flow in God's ways and use music to praise God, it will bring an anointing and a power of the Spirit that we have never experienced. We have sensed it in the church in very special ways as we played and as we sang the music. The Spirit of God was so very evident.

Let me give you an example of this from the Bible. Three kings got together. Two of them were negative, and one of them was good. They needed some help from God, so Jehoshaphat, the good king, called Elisha, the prophet. II Kings 3:13-16 tells us: "And Elisha said unto the king of Israel, What have I to do with thee? Get thee to the prophets of thy father, and to the prophets of thy mother. And the king of Israel said unto him, Nay: for the Lord hath called these three kings together to deliver them into the hand of Moab. And Elisha said, As the Lord of hosts liveth, before whom I stand, surely, were it not that I regard the presence of Jehoshaphat the king of Judah, I would not look toward thee, nor see thee. But now bring me a minstrel. And it came to pass, when the minstrel played, that the hand of the Lord came upon him. And he said, thus saith the Lord ..." In the presence of these evil men, the Spirit of God could not work. Elisha called for a musician, and as the musician played upon his stringed instrument the anointing of God (in the Old Testament it is called the hand of the Lord) came upon the prophet. He began to prophesy about what they should do to win this battle. They did what the prophet said, and they won. It was the ministry of music. It didn't even say a singer. It was just a musician playing an instrument that brought the anointing of the Holy Spirit upon the prophet. People ask, "Why do we sing at the beginning of the service? Why don't we just sing at the end of the service?" It is the music that brings the anointing upon the pastor or the prophet or the teacher or the apostle or the evangelist. That music brings the presence of the Spirit upon the congregation.

Many times we have been watching TV and listening to negative news, so when we come to church we are worrying, or we may have been fighting with the kids. We come in from all different directions and plop down in the meeting place. Many times our minds are not on the Lord. As we begin to sing and minister unto the Lord in music, the anointing begins to flow through the church. We get in one accord and our mind gets centered on the Lord. We are able to receive from the Word and from the gifts of the Spirit. II Chronicles 5:11,12: "It came to pass, when the priests were come out of the holy place: (for all the priests that were present were sanctified, and did not then wait by course: Also the Levites which were the singers, all of them of Asaph, of Heman, of Jeduthun, with their sons and their brethren, being arrayed in white linen, having cymbals and psalteries and harps, stood at the east end of the altar, and with them an hundred and twenty priests sounding with trumpets.)"

Now this is quite an orchestra. This is quite a choir. They have 120 trumpeters, hundreds of singers, harp players, lyre and stringed instrument players, and cymbals. Some of us have to renew our minds because when we think of church music we think of the old funeral march. But that isn't what should be happening here in the temple of God. Do you know what it would sound like with 120 trumpets? Wow! You sure wouldn't need a PA system. II Chronicles 5:13-14: "It came even to pass, as the trumpeters and singers were as one, to make one sound to be heard in praising and thanking the Lord." Notice it said the singers and the musicians were in one accord and all that music was praising and thanking the Lord. Now you may not realize this, but I can get on my drums and praise and thank the Lord without opening my mouth. Just playing the cymbals and drums, I am praising and thanking the Lord. "Oh, Brother Treat, we don't believe in that kind of stuff in our church." Well the Bible says it's all right. Maybe your church should read the Bible. "And when they lifted up their voice with the trumpets and cymbals and instruments of musick, and praised the Lord, saying, For he is good; for his mercy endureth forever; that then the house was filled with a cloud, even the house of the Lord: So that the priests could not stand to minister by reason of the cloud: for the glory of the Lord had filled the house of God." I like that kind of action. As far as I'm concerned, I'd like God to fill our house everyday. Music is a part of that. As we will minister to the Lord in singing, in playing instruments, that music will open the door for the power of God to flow in and fill the house of the Lord with His glory. That's an exciting thing.

Music and praise confuse and defeat the enemy. We have seen people healed during music and praise in the service. Why do you suppose that is? Because, as we ministered to God, the instruments played, the choir sang, all the congregation sang, and the evil spirit that had brought sickness and pain was confused and overcome by the presence of God. He just ran out of there. That has happened in church many times. You don't have to hear bawling and squalling and see rolling on the floor for a demon to be cast out of someone. Music will often just drive the enemy away.

There were some kingdoms which came against Jehoshaphat in II Chronicles 20. The kingdoms of Moab and Amon wanted to destroy God's people and came against Jehoshaphat and the nation. They had a lot more soldiers than Israel had. Israel was in bad shape. Jehoshaphat said, "Let's fast and pray, because there is no way we can fight this battle in the natural." They fasted and prayed, and the prophet stood up and said, "Don't worry about a thing. I am going to fight this battle for you. The battle is the Lord's, not yours. I will overcome, and I will cause you to win." Notice what they did in II Chronicles 20:20-21: "And they rose early in the morning, and went forth into the wilderness of Tekoa: and as they went forth, Jehoshaphat stood and said, Hear me, O Judah, and ye inhabitants of Jerusalem; Believe in the Lord your God, so shall ye be established; believe his prophets, so shall ye prosper. And when he had consulted with the people, he appointed singers unto the Lord, and that should praise the beauty of holiness as they went out before the army, and to say, Praise the Lord; for his mercy endureth forever."

Where were the singers? They went before the army. Can you imagine getting ready to go to battle and putting all the choir members right out in front? Now, in the traditional way of thinking the choir members certainly aren't the most powerful ones in the bunch, but that's what Jehoshaphat did. He put the singers, the musicians, out in front of the army. Look what happened. II Chronicles 20:22: "And when they began to sing and to praise, the Lord set ambushments against the children of Ammon, Moab, and mount Seir, which were come against Judah; and they were smitten." When did that happen? When they began to sing and to praise. Perhaps you haven't developed your praise life yet. If you haven't made singing, praising, and worshipping the Lord a daily part of your life, then you should, because when you are worshipping and singing unto the Lord Satan cannot stay in your presence. The enemy flee and is smitten in your presence. A lot of people are struggling with the Lord. If you'll just praise and worship God, those things will be taken care of and you won't need to struggle. Psalm 9:1-3 says: "I will praise thee, O lord, with my whole heart; I will shew forth all thy marvelous works. I will be glad and rejoice in thee: I will sing praise to thy name, O thou most High. When mine enemies are turned back, they shall fall and perish at thy presence."

The psalmist is saying, "As I am praising thee, as I am worshipping and singing unto thee, the enemy will be turned back, and he will fall and perish at thy presence." Remember, God inhabits the praise of Israel. God is present in our praise, and the enemy is defeated in the presence of God.

In Acts 16, Paul and Silas had been taken captive. They were locked up in jail, bound hand and foot. What did they do? They prayed and sang praises. As they did, God sent ambushments against the enemies, shook that prison with an earthquake, threw the doors open, and everyone's bands were loosed. When? When they were singing praises to the Lord. Many of you have been struggling in the areas of depression, sickness, poverty, or problems in your home. If you will begin to fill your life with praise, those things will be driven out of your life and you will find victory.

Satan uses music to bring evil because he knows its power and effect. God uses music to bring good and to stop evil. The longest book of the Bible is a list of songs and instructions for praise and worship. That should tell you something. When you come to church, you will see about 20 percent of the congregation really involved with praise and worship. The reason that more people are not receiving the gifts and blessings and power of God is because they are not entering in. You can pray till your tongue falls out, but if you don't start praising and worshipping the Lord you are never going to drive the evil out of your life. The presence of God is never going to be with you on a consistent basis.

You say, "Oh, Brother Treat, that is so sissy." Do you suppose that's what the prisoners did when Paul and Silas sang the glory of God into the jail house, caused an earthquake, and turned them all loose? Do you suppose they said, "Paul you are such a sissy, causing earthquakes"? Do you suppose they called David a sissy when he was worshipping and singing praises to God, when the anointing would come upon him to drive the enemies out of his presence? David ruled over the greatest nation that has ever existed. Do you suppose they called him a sissy?

I don't think they called Jehoshaphat a sissy when he put the choir out in front of the troops and they worshipped and sang, "The Lord is good and his mercy endureth forever," and all the enemy was defeated. The Bible says it took them three days to pick up all the spoils. They just took all the wealth of those countries and went back to Jerusalem blessed and prosperous. I don't suppose they called them sissies. A sissy is one who doesn't have the guts to obey the Word of God. A mighty man of valor or a mighty woman of valor is one who will stand up, do what God's Word says, and not care what anybody thinks about it.

We must decide to follow God's guidelines and instructions for worship, not our own ideas or traditions. Psalm 34:1 says: "I will bless the Lord at all times: his praise shall continually be in my mouth." If we praise God continually, there won't be time to worry, gripe, complain, and murmur. We won't have time to gossip. Praise will be continually in our mouths.

God wants us to sing and praise in the congregation. Here are just a few guidelines concerning praise and worship we need to be aware of. Psalm 22:22: "I will declare thy name unto my brethren: in the midst of the congregation will I praise thee."

A lot of people say, "You don't have to go to church to be a Christian," or "You don't have to go to church regularly to be a good Christian," but you do. You do! There is no way you could obey the Bible and not be committed to a local church on a daily basis. The Bible tells us to praise God in the midst of the congregation. You can't do that at home. You need to be involved with the congregation on a regular basis so that you can praise God like the Bible teaches. Psalms 35:18: "I will give thee thanks in the great congregation: I will praise thee among much people."

Give God thanks in the congregation. Praise Him among the people. "Well, Brother Treat, I get nervous with all those people around me." Well, thank God you have an opportunity to work through that fear and obey the scriptures. You've overcome nervousness before, and you can overcome it again to do what the Bible says. Lift up your hands, give God praise and worship in the midst of the congregation. Corporate worship and praise is a special thing which no one in the world can relate to except the members of the body of Christ. Out there in the world they have no idea what it is to stand with a group of people and praise God. When you come into a church that obeys the scriptures concerning music, worship, and praise you are experiencing a very, very special thing. Psalms 96:1-3 says: "O sing unto the Lord a new song: sing unto the Lord, all the earth. Sing unto the Lord, bless his name; shew forth his salvation from day to day. Declare his glory among the heathen, his wonders among all people." We should be ready to worship God and to praise God among all people at any time.

God desires for us to clap and lift up our hands. I specifically put this in here because a lot of people come from the "first church of the Frigidaire." There are many people who are a part of the "frozen chosen," so they get nervous when you start clapping and praising the Lord the way the Bible says. We want to do what the Bible says. We're not interested in how people think about us. We are interested in what God said. Psalms 63:4: "Thus will I bless thee while I live: I will lift up my hands in thy name." Isn't that clear and simple? He didn't say, "Fold thine arms." He said, "Lift up thy hands." Psalms 47:1: "Oh clap your hands, all ye people..." Sometimes the Spirit of God is so strong in church I can't do anything but clap my hands. "Oh, Brother Treat, I went to your church, and you are so irreverent. Why, there's clapping in there like they're in some kind of football game or something." No, we're just obeying the Bible. We are doing what God commanded. He said, "Clap your hands all ye people." That wasn't a suggestion; that was the Word of God. "Shout unto God with a voice of triumph." (Psalms 47:1) Some Christians have never obeyed that scripture. They are so reserved and such a prim and proper Christian that they won't do what the Bible says.

Shout unto God. Shout unto God with a voice of triumph! It didn't say to whisper unto God with a voice of misery and heartache. The average congregation during worship and praise mumbles, if they will do anything at all. Is that true?

When I was growing up, I never entered a church where they would shout unto God with a voice of triumph and clapped their hands. I believe that is one reason why I wasn't interested in churches. There was no power of God there. There was no presence of the Lord there, just religious tradition. You say, "Well, Brother Treat, do all churches have to do that?" No, just the ones that want to obey the Bible. Some churches just come right out and tell you, "We are not interested in what the Bible has to say; we have our own traditions." But those who want to follow the Bible are going to clap their hands and shout to God with a voice of triumph. Psalms 134:1-3: "Behold, bless ye the Lord, all ye servants of the Lord, which by night stand in the house of the Lord. Lift up your hands in the sanctuary, and bless the Lord. The Lord that made heaven and earth bless thee out of Zion." God desires for us to praise Him boldly and loudly. Psalms 98:4-6: "Make a joyful noise unto the Lord, all the earth: make a loud noise..."

There is no way to spiritualize this or give it some deeper meaning, it simply means, "Make a loud noise." If you want to get a cymbal and make a loud noise, do it. "Brother Treat, I can't see how a Christian could play the drums and call it worship." That's all it said, make a loud noise and rejoice and sing praise. "Sing unto the Lord with the harp; with the harp, and the voice of a psalm. With trumpets and sound of cornets make a joyful noise before the Lord, the King." You get a bunch of trumpets, cornets, harps, and cymbals together, and you have some noise! The devil lied to us when he told us that to be spiritual you have to be quiet. The devil put in our minds that the concept of spirituality is quietness; to really get close to God is to go to a monastery or some place far away from people where you can be quiet. "If you really want to be spiritual, you have to walk quietly into church like you're walking on egg shells. Just slip into church and slip into your pew." That's not what God said to do. He said, "Get the cornets, get the trumpets, get out the strings, and let's jam!" Spirituality is not quiet.

Now there are times when we are quiet before the Lord, and some of us Pentecostals need to learn that scripture, too. There are times when we are quiet before the Lord and we meditate. It is a positive thing to do, and it should be a part of our spiritual life, but most of us don't have any problem

being quiet. Most of us have never experienced
these scriptures of praise and making a loud noise
before the Lord. God wants us to do that. God is
seeking for us to do that. God is desiring for people
to do that. Maybe you need to break through your
spiritual cell. Any instruments that have been
invented can be used to praise the Lord.

God desires His people to dance before Him in
praise and worship. Here's a strong area you can
renew your mind in. I know many of you are just
stiff as a board when you worship and praise. You
have to renew your mind to the scriptures. "Yeah,
but, Brother Treat, I'm afraid I might look funny."
You're not praising me. I don't care how you look.
You're not praising the people around you. They
shouldn't worry about how you look either. You're
praising God, and God likes the way you look. You
used to get out there and dance around for your
sweetheart. You jump up and down for a football
team. Why not dance before God? Psalms 149:1-3
says: "Praise ye the Lord. Sing unto the Lord a new
song, and his praise in the congregation of saints.
Let Israel rejoice in him that made him: let the children of Zion be joyful in their King. Let them praise
his name in the dance: let them sing praises unto
him with the timbrel and harp." Praise his name in
the dance. You need to just cut loose. You need to
quit being so nervous and uptight. Get rid of your
fear. The devil binds you up. The devil's been telling you, "Oh don't do that. You look funny, and you
might fall down. You might do something stupid."
That's just the devil trying to keep you from obeying the scriptures. Do you know what the devil

knows? He knows if you will begin to praise God and dance before the Lord freely and openly you'll have such an anointing, a freedom, and a liberty come on your life that you will be a powerful vessel of the glory of God, and the devil doesn't want you to do that. He wants you to stay uptight, proper, and nervous in church.

In II Samuel 6:14, David was bringing the Ark of the Covenant into Jerusalem. The Bible said that David danced before the Lord with all of his might. In Hebrew it means he threw a fit. He was dancing before God with everything he had. He did it right down in the middle of the streets of Jerusalem. He was dancing and praising God in front of everybody. His wife was like some of us. His wife said, "Well, you sure did make a fool out of yourself today, Dave, dancing in front of all those people. Some king you are." Do you know what happened? She was cursed and never bore children. Don't look down your nose when some sister comes by you skipping and dancing before the Lord or when some brother is jumping and praising God. Don't look down your nose, or you might get the same "fruit" that Michal got when she looked down her nose at David. I don't say that to threaten. I'm just making you aware of what the Bible says. If the Bible said it, let's get with it. I don't ask myself how I feel about it. I'm just going to do what the Word says. Psalms 30:11: "Thou hast turned for me my mourning into dancing..."

When you really get involved with the presence of God, your nervousness, your sadness, will be turned into dancing. Someone said, "Yeah, but what if we do it in the flesh?" You have a body. How are you going to get out of the flesh? As long as we are doing it toward the Lord, to worship and praise the Lord, God accepts it. God enjoys it. God desires it. That old concept of the quiet little church mouse is not Biblical. There isn't anything spiritual about it. Some people want you to think they are really spiritual, so they just talk ever so softly. I want to throw up when I get around people like that. There isn't anything spiritual about it. I have them come to me all the time and whisper, "Brother Treat, the Lord has shared some things with me." Go change your voice, and maybe I'll listen to it. That's not God. That's not spirituality. Do you suppose, when you get to heaven, God is going to whisper, "I'm so glad you all came"? The Bible said God's voice is like thunder. When Jesus spoke, thousands could hear without a PA system. Luke 19:37-40 says: "And when he was come nigh, even now at the descent of the Mount of Olives, the whole multitude of the disciples began to rejoice and praise God with a loud voice for all the mighty works that they had seen; Saying, Blessed be the King that cometh in the name of the Lord: peace in heaven, and glory in the highest. And some of the Pharisees from among the multitude said unto him, Master, rebuke thy disciples. And he answered and said unto them, I tell you that, if these should hold their peace, the stones would immediately cry out." I tell you, I don't want to be replaced with a rock. I want to do what the Word of God says or God's going to get a rock to replace me. No, Lord. I'll do it.

God desires musical instruments to be used in

praise and worship. A lot of people have hang-ups with musical instruments in church. The Bible teaches us to use musical instruments. Jesus never said, "Don't do it." Psalm 150:1-6 says: "Praise ye the Lord, Praise God in his sanctuary: praise him in the firmament of his power. Praise him for his mighty acts: praise him according to his excellent greatness. Praise him with the sound of the trumpet: praise him with the psaltery and harp. Praise him with timbrel and dance: praise him with stringed instruments and organs. Praise him upon the loud cymbals: praise him upon the high sounding cymbals. Let everything that hath breath praise the Lord. Praise ye the Lord." You read it; now do it. Praise the Lord!

8
Successful Family Life

Y ou might be wondering why I would include
family life as a chapter in a Christian Foundations book when the main purpose of this
book is to establish basic doctrines of the Bible. If
your family life is not in order, then you are not
going to be a successful Christian.

It's important that we line our lives up with the
Word of God in our homes. Many people have this
attitude: "Church is for church. Home is for home.
Business is for business. Don't mix them up. I'm
going to do what I want to do; and as long as I don't
do it in church, what do you care?"

See, most people don't want a Christian life style,
not a seven-day-a-week, 24-hour-a-day, walking-
with-God-all-the-time life style. To be a successful
Christian, though, that is exactly the kind of desire
you must have.

A very basic part of the Christian life style is to
have your home life in order. First let's take a look
at marriage. God instituted marriage to provide
the fullest life possible for men and women. Look at
Genesis 2:18-20: "And the Lord God said, It is not

good that the man should be alone; I will make him an help meet for him. And out of the ground the Lord God formed every beast of the field, and every fowl of the air; and brought them unto Adam to see what he would call them: and whatsoever Adam called every living creature, that was the name thereof. And Adam gave names to all cattle, and to the fowl of the air, and to every beast of the field; but for Adam there was not found an help meet for him." Notice that all the animals were there, but there wasn't a help meet or a companion or a partner for Adam. The Bible said God created all the beasts and Adam was standing there all by himself saying, "There is no one here for me." That meant he had to lower himself to turn to animals for companionship. Folks, dog is not man's best friend!

It's sad, but to a lot of people their animals are more important than other people. They'll take their poodle to the hair salon and get them a perm, they'll take them out for a walk, brush them, bathe them, buy them a sweater. It is serious when they will pay more attention to their dog than they do their spouse. I know some people who have horses. They love their horses. They talk to their horses, clean the horse's stall, wash the horses, rub the horses, ride the horses. They spend 10 times more time with the horses than they do with their spouse. Isn't that sad?

When I was in the world, I used to have this dog. I'd say, "You're the only one who really understands me. You'd love me no matter what I did; wouldn't you?" I would just talk to that dog and lay my head on it and cry. You have to lower yourself to turn to animals for companionship. But God said, "I'm going to create a companion for Adam." Genesis 2:21-23: "And the Lord God caused a deep sleep to fall upon Adam and he slept: and he took one of his ribs, and closed up the flesh instead thereof; And the rib, which the Lord God had taken from man, made he a woman, and brought her unto the man. And Adam said, This is now bone of my bones, and flesh of my flesh: she shall be called Woman, because she was taken out of Man." The woman was taken out of man. The man was formed from the dust of the ground, and God breathed into his nostrils the breath of life. But God didn't go through the same process to create a woman. He took the woman out of the man.

There have been many things that have been done incorrectly in the area of authority and women. In some religious systems, women have been dominated in a way that is not Biblical. In worldly systems today, the women rebel. They rise up and try to be men. Both are wrong, but we still have to recognize the fact, that while God created the man, He took the woman out of the man. Eve was the helpmate for Adam. She was not created for herself. God didn't go over to the woman and say, "I'm going to create a helpmeet for you." He said that to the man. The woman was taken out of the man. You just can't change that. That shouldn't make women feel bad or down or low. That's the way God designed it. A women has her part in God's plan even as a man has his part in God's plan. One is not lower than the other. They are just different. When a man tries to be a woman, he's in trouble. And, when a woman tries to be a man, she's in trouble. But, when we'll all do what God created us to do, we'll win. I'm glad men are men and women are women. I'm glad I'm a man, and I am glad that Wendy's a woman—really glad. As long as we both function as God created us to, we'll have a beautiful life. God established this life.

God instituted marriage, and He said it is not good that man be alone. That's why He brought the two together. Look at Genesis 2:24-25: "Therefore shall a man leave his father and his mother, and shall cleave unto his wife: and they shall be one flesh. And they were both naked, the man and his wife, and were not ashamed." God never changed His plan. God never came along and said, "Well, it would be better if you all stayed single." It's still a fact that it's not good for man to be alone; it's not good for woman to be alone. God instituted marriage for men and women to live the fullest possible life.

Let me just add this for the single folks: There are situations where you may live a life as a single person. That's not the norm and I don't believe it's something you should desire, but if you are in that position and that's what works best for you, then just do what God has called you to do. Enjoy His blessing as He has established your life.

Some of you single people, because of guilt, past problems, bitterness, and other circumstances, have arranged your lives in such a way that you are rejecting God's best. Don't resist marriage; don't reject it. It's a sad thing when you have a bunch of married people who wish they weren't and a bunch of single people who wish they were. Let's just get on the Word of God and live the best. Marriage provides a basis for growth and fulfillment spiritually, mentally, and physically. Marriage will definitely help you grow. Either that or you'll go buggy!

Let's turn to Matthew 19:4: "And he answered and said unto them, Have ye not read, that he which made them at the beginning made them male and female." There's no third sex in there. You are either a male or a female, *period!* There's no other part. There's no other thing you can come up with. God made them male and female. What about the homosexuals? What about the lesbians? They're just sinners; that's all. They need to get saved and repent like everybody else. God didn't make them that way. God made them male or female. God's not confused about it. He didn't make a mistake. There are men trying to have operations to make themselves women, and women having operations to make themselves men. All of that is sin. Any doctor who gets involved with that is in sin. Any person who gets involved with that is in sin. Now, that doesn't make them any worse off than a drunkard or a liar or a thief. They're not in some supernaturally evil condition. They're just in the same sin the rest of the world is in. Sometimes we look at them as "real bad." They're in the same spot all of us were in before we got born again. They need to get saved. The same salvation that helped us will help them. God brings men and women together and causes them to be one flesh.

Matthew 19:5-6 says: "And said, For this cause shall a man leave father and mother, and shall cleave to his wife: and they twain shall be one flesh? Wherefore they are no more twain, but one flesh. What therefore God hath joined together, let not man put asunder." That doesn't mean men and women are one soul. Your soul is your mind, your emotions, and your will. When you get married, you don't have one mind and one emotional makeup and one will. There are still two of you. That's where you get to grow because you both think the same way you did before you were married, and this is where the problems come in. He's always wrong, and she's always right, or the other way around. This is where we get to grow.

Anytime you make a decision to spend your life with another person, you have a challenge on your hands. Just think about it. How many of you have gone on a vacation with another family before? When you make the decision to take a week and spend it with that other family, you have a challenge on your hands. Now the first day is no problem. You can do anything for a day, but after three or four days you are on each others nerves unless you know how to change and grow and talk and give so you can continue to flow in harmony. How many times have you been with somebody for an extended period of time and after it was over you said, "I'll tell you what; that will be the last time we do that with them." Anytime you get hooked up with somebody else, you have a challenge on your hands.

If you and I are going out to dinner, we have the challenge to relate to one another, to communicate to one another, and to enjoy that time together. We could end up mad, throwing water on each other and walking out. That happens. When a man and a woman decide to live a lifetime together, man, you talk about a challenge! Everyday you are going to have to deal with one another. You're going to have to learn how to communicate, share, help, and be involved with each other. You have a challenge. That's why marriage provides the most opportunity for growth. A lot of people want to stay single because they don't want to hassle with changing. They want to do what they want, how they want, and when they want without consulting anyone else. If they were married, they'd mess up that other person with their lousy attitude. But God knows how you can grow to be your best, and that's why He instituted marriage.

The Word gives guidelines for a good marriage partner. If you follow the Word, you will be smart. Just because the first time you saw her your heart fluttered and a voice said, "This is the one," does not mean she is really the one. If you base your marriage on your emotions or on a sign or on some dream you'll probably fail. About half of all marriages go up in smoke because most people do not base their marriages on the Word of God; they base it on how they feel. Their marriage is not based on love or the Word of God or the truth or commitment; therefore, it is going to end up in disaster.

Divorce is clearly not the Will of God, but is also not the unpardonable sin. It's not a bigger thing for God to forgive than theft or drinking or smoking or anything else. If you have gone through a divorce, you should not go through guilt and condemnation over it as it's no more difficult for God to forgive that than those other things. In God's eyes it's all the same. The thing that's more complicated about divorce, is that you can change things like smoking a little easier than you can change the things that bring about divorce.

You know once you do something one time it's easier to do it the second time. Once you do it the second time, it's easier to do it the third time. So you must be sure to change those things that lead to divorce so it doesn't come up again. Let's look at some things that will describe to us a good marriage partner.

1.) ***The person must be a believer.*** Now, for you single people, if you are dating or even considering dating a person who is not a believer, don't waste your time. You can help them get saved, but don't think about dating them. If you say, "Well, I'll marry him, and then he'll get saved," you need to have your head examined. If he won't get born again before, what makes you think he's going to get saved afterward? He got what he wanted, so why mess around with this church stuff? Even around "Word churches," places teaching the Bible, we just seem to have a lot of people who are very foolish in the area of dating non-Christians, trying to build a relationship with someone who is on their way to hell, under the dominance of the devil, and a child of disobedience.

Parents, this is something you should be very strongly teaching your children. If they even think about dating an unborn again person, red lights should start flashing in their brains and signs come up in front of their eyes so they will turn and walk away.

You can tell if someone is a believer or not. People who just go to church are not believers. A lot of people who sit in church don't believe anything. When they walk out of church, they act like a sinner. Their attitude is bad, thinking is bad, behavior is bad. The first thing in thinking about a marriage relationship is your mate must be a believer. Find somebody who has the same spirit you have, somebody who has the same plan for life you have, based on the Word of God, somebody who has the same God you have, somebody who has the same eternity you have. If you're on your way to heaven and he's on his way to hell, that's going to be a tough life. You'll wake up happy; he'll wake up sad. Everyday you'll be praising God, and he'll be worried. How can you get along like that?

Now, for those of you who are married and your spouse is not a Christian, don't hound him and bother him into the kingdom of heaven. It won't work. Make it your top priority to show him such an example of Christian love and Christian life and Christian power that he can't resist it. Then he'll come on in and be a part of the family of God.

Study I Peter 3:1-7. You'll find out that you *can* win your spouse without preaching to him. Not always, but usually, it's the man who is not saved and the woman is, and some of you women have done more to keep your husbands away from God than any other cause. If you'll just show that Christian love, that life, and that power, he'll come in. He doesn't want to hear you preaching, but if he can see the life and power he'll come on in.

The primary ingredient for a successful marriage relationship is that you two are believers. That doesn't mean you can't have any fun or any good things out of marriage if you are married to an unbeliever, but being a believer is the primary ingredient.

2.) *You must be in agreement with your beliefs and goals.* If you are Spirit filled and you are married to a person who says, "Well, I'm a Christian, but I don't believe in that tongues stuff," you're not going to get along very well. If you find a lady and she's a good Christian but she believes that God wants her to suffer and you believe what the Bible says about healing, you aren't going to get along very well. If any symptom comes up, you'll rebuke it in the name of Jesus and drive it out, but she'll try to catch it and hang on to it. You'll be overcoming in the name of Jesus, and she'll be suffering in the name of Jesus. You won't be in agreement. Your beliefs and your goals will be completely different. You would be believing to prosper, and she would be believing to fail. You must find someone who has the same beliefs and goals you do.

When I say "goals," I'm talking about your direction in life. You're sold out to Jesus, and you're ready to do whatever the Lord tells you to do. If He says, "I want you to go over to the Philippines for two weeks and preach the gospel" and you're ready to go, but your spouse throws a fit about it, you are not in agreement about your goals. You must establish your goals for life right off the bat. What are your goals? Where are you headed? Are you just living to work from nine to five and get a paycheck, to buy a car every couple of years and try to get your house paid off and keep groceries in your cupboard? Are those your only goals? Is the greatest thrill in your life when you get to go to Disneyland? Or is your eternal goal to retire, to get yourself a camper and go out with Smokey the Bear? Praise God people can retire and go camping; but, if that's the greatest goal you have, I'll tell you right now, you and I wouldn't get along very well. We couldn't flow together because those are not my goals.

A lot of people get married and don't even think about where they are going. They don't even think about their goals. The husband has his mind set in one direction. His goal is to get himself a 28-foot yacht and bob around out there like a cork. She has another goal and is motivated and pushing for something else. Life goes by, and they get farther and farther apart. That's how divorce comes about after 20 or 30 years of marriage. They never established an agreement on their beliefs or their goals.

Some of you have been married for awhile, and you never have sat down and talked about this. I'm stirring you up now to go ahead and do it. Sit down and write out where you are headed. What are you doing around here anyway? What are your goals? Do you want to be a part of the ministry? Do you want to get to the place where you are financially able to travel to minister in other countries or to help other ministries? Where do you want to be? If your goal is to get a bigger house, that's not too satisfying. If your biggest goal is to get the lawn mowed on Saturday, your life is pretty dry. You need to talk about those things. You need to agree on them. Amos 3:3 says: "Can two walk together except they be agreed?"

3.) ***Must not be quarrelsome or given to strife.*** Proverbs 21:9: "It is better to dwell in a corner of the housetop, than with a brawling woman in a wide house." I don't know why He said "woman," but He did. I'll just go along with the Lord. Of course it applies both ways. There are people who are flexible and will go with the flow, and there are people who are brawlers. They just want their own way. That type of an individual will not be a good spouse. You will spend your whole life doing what they want.

Find an individual who is not quarrelsome or given to strife. Some people feel bad if they don't have something to fight about every day. They feel like they are missing something. Everything might be going well, but they'll find something to fight about. People think "Let's just fight to make sure you still love me and so we can make up." Squabbling and quarreling is just not God's way. We think that if we smile pretty on Sunday no one will know that we have fought all the way to church and probably for the better part of the week. That is sad. What makes it even worse is the fact that if we would be honest with ourselves most of the time we don't even know what we are mad and upset about. We will go for days not speaking to each other, and we don't know what we are mad about. We just know we're *mad.*

Once Wendy and I were arguing. (I said only once) In the middle of the argument, I thought to myself, "This is stupid, but I'm not going to stop now because I'm already into this thing, and I know I'm right." So I just kept right on going. Now, that's the devil. If you would take a look at some of the things you have been squabbling about, you'd realize it is an evil spirit coming in to divide your home.

I'm trying to tell you some truth here. It's not that you're bad. It's not that your spouse is bad, but we have an enemy. The devil sends demon spirits to divide homes, especially Christian homes that have the potential of serving God and winning others to Jesus. The devil is going to do everything he can to split you up, ruin your testimony, ruin your kids' lives, and mess everything up. He'll send a demon to stir up strife and quarreling. You really don't have anything against each other, but that demon gets in there, and you just get mad. Now, if you're wise you'll say, "I'm not going to let that demon control me. I'm not going to let those demons come in and break up my home." Start praying and keep those demons out. When a bad attitude flares up, when those thoughts peep into your mind, rebuke and resist them. Continue to walk in love, and you'll work things out. Realize that when you are involved in quarreling and fighting you have a demon spirit in your house and you have to drive him out. Find a partner who is not quarrelsome and given to strife. If you have a quarrelsome partner now, love them until they renew their mind.

4.) *Must be willing to change or renew their mind.* None of us have it all together, that means if we are going to have a successful partnership both of us are going to be changing and growing, improving and renewing our minds. Romans 12:2 says, "We are transformed by the renewing of our mind to do the will of God." If you have a person who is willing to change, then you have a person who is unlimited. Your relationship is unlimited because you'll both be growing and changing all your lives. By the time you are 100 or 110 years old, you're going to know some things! If you don't change, when you get to be old, you'll be the same way you were when you were 30 or 40. Now you're just slower at it. The attitude is the same, the behavior is the same. You think the same way because you never decided to be changing and growing and renewing your mind. Ten years from now I want to be different than I am right now. Twenty years from now I want to be a lot different than I am right now. When I'm 70 I really want to be different than I am right now, and I don't mean that I am going to be slower. I want to be different in my thinking, different in my attitude, different in my behavior.

5.) ***Must be responsible and disciplined.*** Don't marry a sluggard. If the guy picks you up in the car and you have to brush the trash out of the way to get in, you've got a problem. That is the way his house is going to look. If he pulls open his drawer and starts digging like a dog looking for a bone, you've got trouble. You say, "Brother Treat, what difference does your drawer make?" Your drawer will tell me what's going on inside you. You open a guy's closet, and I'll tell you how his mind works. If stuff is just piled in a big mess, that's how his mind works. His mind is just scrambled up. You look at a woman's cupboards in her kitchen, and you'll find out how her mind is working. If you open up that cupboard and say, "OOOOOHHHHHHHH!!!!!" that will tell you she is confused. Find somebody who is disciplined. Find somebody who is orderly. Find somebody who has their life under control.

II Timothy 1:7 says: "For God hath not given us the spirit of fear; but of power, and of love, and of a sound mind." The words "sound mind" mean a disciplined, orderly mind. God wants people to be disciplined and orderly. Just because you're a Christian doesn't mean you are supposed to cut your head off and act like a fool. Christians should be the sharpest, the wisest, the most knowledgeable, the most clear, the most plugged-in people. A lot of us have the idea, "I'm saved. I'm just going to follow my spirit." That isn't walking by faith! That is foolishness. "Jesus is made unto me *wisdom.*" So find someone who is disciplined and responsible, especially when you plan to have children.

You don't want the type of guy who would tell you, the wife, to change the baby. You want a guy who is responsible and will get up and take care of the baby right along with you. I never could figure out why a wife would ask her husband to baby-sit. Now that is dingy. He's the parent. The wife should say, "I'm going to be gone this week. What are you going to do with the baby?" It's as much his responsibility as it is hers. Nine times out of ten, when the kid needs something mama jumps up to do it. He says, "Wife, did you get the baby-sitter? It's your responsibility." Find me a scripture on that!

Those five things are guidelines for a good marriage partner. None of us are fully developed in those areas. They are things we should be working with and growing with. Find somebody who is responsible and disciplined. That person will make you a good spouse. If you are married right now and you see you haven't been responsible and disciplined...change. Some of you men would leave your head at home if it wasn't for your wife. Be responsible. Be disciplined. Be a team. Somebody may look at those five guidelines and think, "I ain't never going to find me a spouse." You don't have to be perfect. None of us are perfect. But these are areas we want to grow in and work on.

Marriage must be entered into with the right motive; to give our love and share our life with the other person. Most of us had wrong motives when we got married. But thank God motives can change. When I got saved it was out of the fear of what would happen if I didn't get saved. I had to change that motive if I wanted to grow with God. God doesn't give us a spirit of fear. If I wanted to grow with God, I couldn't be there because of fear. Somewhere along the line in my Christian walk I had to change that motive and say, "Father, I am here now because I love you. I give my life to you. I desire to walk with you."

You might have gotten married for any number of reasons, but right now examine yourself and make sure that you stay married because you love that person and you desire to give your life to that individual. You're not there to get. If you are there to get, you will destroy the marriage. "I never get a thing from him." You're destroying your marriage with that attitude. When you give you will receive.

When you seek to get, you will destroy. Jesus said, "Give and it shall be given unto you." If you got married for any motive other than love, just say this to yourself. "I'm going to change that motive right now. I'm here to love and I desire to give myself." That will solve a lot of your problems. Love must be our motive.

Negative motives will destroy a relationship. Romance or emotions are not going to last very long. Romance can be enjoyed in your relationship, but it will not keep your marriage together. At six o'clock in the morning when your hair is in every direction and the make-up is gone, the romance isn't too strong. When financial pressures are on and strife sets in, romance is not a part of that. If romance is the only thing holding you together, then you don't really have a thing. You all know how romance comes and goes. It is not a good basis for a marriage. It is a fleeting thing.

Physical looks won't hold you together either. He or she might put on 15 pounds. What are you going to do then? You could find somebody who looks better. What are you going to do then? You can have the most beautiful little creature, but she can be the most cantankerous thing that her looks will be overshadowed by her attitude. In fact, most of the time people who want to be Mr. Universe are pretty dingy in the head. Now I said *most* of the time, so if you consider yourself Mr. Universe you may be an exception. In my experience in dating and being around all kinds of people, the people who don't always look like they just stepped off the cover of a fashion magazine, are more human than Mr. or

Mrs. Perfect.

I'll tell you why some of you brothers have been having problems. You've been out there looking for model types, but the body wears out quickly and there's no reality there. Then you wonder why you're not enjoying it, and you keep going from one to another to another. Why don't you start looking for a human being instead of a body?

Some of you women just have to find a guy with a certain kind of shoulders and a certain kind of hair and a certain kind of looks, and then you really know he's the right one. The guy might be loonier than a cartoon. He's been pumping iron and eating steroids. That's not the kind of guy you need. He can lift 300 pounds, but he can't think his way out of a paper bag.

As for sex, that's not a reason to get married. People come up pregnant. "Well, we're pregnant. We've got to get married." Listen, just because you are pregnant, don't add a divorce to it. If you are getting married just because she is pregnant, you probably are not going to last very long. Now, if you have a good relationship and can make a commitment and really want to be married, that's good, but don't do it because of the pregnancy.

If loneliness is your motive, the marriage won't last very long. Wanting to get away from parents, will wear off quickly, too. It's the same with wanting someone to take care of you. I hear people say, "Brother Treat, I just want someone who will cook my meals and wash my clothes and take care of me. Is that too much to ask?" It isn't going to work. I'd give that marriage a year. A lot of times people get married because they want to have children, but that won't work, either.

Another compelling force is peer pressure. "Everybody else is married. My best friend is married. Well, I guess I had better get married, too."

Have you ever noticed how marriages and births run in cycles? There will be a flood of marriages and a flood of babies. It's kind of a peer pressure thing. Everybody's doing it. It's the "in" thing now a days. But it doesn't work. A couple of years after I left high school, several of my buddies were getting married. I didn't get married till five years after I left high school, and by that time most of them were divorced. They got married for all the wrong motives. It didn't last.

In marriage the two must live as one. Although you are individuals and you always will be individuals, don't try to dominate each other and take away that individuality, but you have to learn how to function as a unit. You learn to function as a unit, not as separate individuals. If you're single, don't get married if you don't want to be a part of a team.

In marriage, neither person is more important or bigger than the other. You are equal. So you need to function as a team. You work together spiritually, mentally, and physically. Do you look to your spouse to help you, or do you do everything you can to let them know you don't need them? You might not use those words, but that's the message a lot of us get. We think "Well, I can carry this burden on my own." Then we have these thoughts or conversations like this. "What's wrong?" "Nothing!" What's the message? "Something's wrong, but I'm not going to tell you because I don't need you. I am not on your team, and you are not on my team, so just leave me alone." "Is there something I can help you with, Honey?" "No, it's all right. Never mind." This kind of behavior destroys marriages. "Well, I just can't tell my husband these things. There are just some things you have to hold to yourself." That destroys a marriage. Rosey Grier once said, "Team work is what breeds success."

The team is what will win. The individual will always lose. If a team member cannot share his weaknesses and his needs with the rest of the team, then the person and the team will be defeated, I guarantee you. A team full of people where each is trying to be a star in his own right is a losing team. You must learn to function as a team. You must be able to go to one another and say, "Let's pray about this. I need you to agree with me. I need you to intercede with me about this." Don't have the attitude, "Well, I'm going to take care of this on my own, bless God." God designed you to work together, not to be separate. He said, "It's not good that you be alone." Just because you are in the same house doesn't mean that you work together. It seems like the men usually have the most difficulty in this area, and some of you men are tearing up your homes because you will not submit to your wife. "Submit to my wife! She's supposed to submit to me." Well, you forgot to read the verse before that. Paul said, "Submitting one to another." If you never submit one to the other, you never function as a team. You need to function spiritually, mentally, and physically as a team.

You need to communicate. Ephesians 4:29 says:
"Let no corrupt communication proceed out of your
mouth, but that which is good to the use of edifying,
that it may minister grace unto the hearers." You
know you usually talk to other people in a nicer
manner than you talk to your wife or husband.
That's a sad thing. You wouldn't talk to me the way
you do your spouse. At least you better not! You say
words to each other that are so destructive and so
hurtful. Some of you are professional knife-
throwers with your tongue. That's a sad thing. The
Bible said, "Speak that which is edifying, ministers grace to the hearer." Matthew 5:37 says: "But
let your communication be, Yea, yea; Nay, nay: for
whatsoever is more than these cometh of evil." You
know what that's all about; don't you?

See, the problem a lot of relationships have is
they really don't know what the other person
wants. This is always such a good example: "Where
do you want to eat?" "I don't care." "Okay, let's go
eat Mexican." "No." "I thought you said you didn't
care." "Yeah, but I don't want to go there." "Okay,
let's go eat Chinese." "No, I don't want to go there
either." "Well, do you or don't you want to go out to
eat?" Here's another good example: Husbands, you
should let your wife know what you think. "Do you
like my hair, Honey?" "Oh, yeah. Isn't it the same
as always?" "No, I just cut off six inches and had a
perm." "Oh, it's nice." That's sad. Communicate
clearly to each other. Say what you mean and mean
what you say. If you want to lie on the couch and be a
sluggard, then say, "I want to lie on the couch and
be a sluggard. That's what I want to do. Don't bug

me while I slug around." If you will begin to speak
what is really there, then you can begin to work
together.

What do you suppose would happen if all the football team members got in the huddle and said,
"Okay, quarterback, what play are we going to
do?" "Oh I don't care. Let's just do whatever you all
want." So they go back to the line of scrimmage and
one guy takes off for a pass, another goes for a
reverse, the other guy goes for a quarterback
sneak, another guy goes off for something else, and
the quarterback gets creamed, and they lose yard-
age. The whole team got in a mess because the
quarterback couldn't make a decision. He couldn't
say "yes" or "no." A lot of what brings defeat to the
home is that people won't let their yea be yea and
their nay be nay.

Here are some basic areas of communication.
These are areas that you really need to get a hold of:

Sex. "Oh, Brother Treat, I'm so embarrassed."
Well, it's time that you grow up. It's time you quit
playing little kiddie games. You're not a teenager
in the back seat of a car. You're husband and wife,
and you need to start talking.

Money. You need to talk about money before you
go out and do your own thing. You don't go out and
spend all the money and then just wait until she
asks you about it. "Well, Honey, what happened to
the money?" "Don't you know?" Would she be ask-
ing you if she knew? "Well, I *thought* you knew."
"The bills have come in. Now what do you expect
me to do?" That's not communication. You're trying
to cover up and hide things from your spouse. My

wife, Wendy, used to sell shoes. Women would say to her, "Boy, I like these shoes. You know, I could buy these and just stick them in the closet for a couple of weeks, and my husband would never know it. Then when I get them out he will say, 'When did you get those?' And I can say, 'Oh, I've had these for a long time.' " That's wrong. That's lying. Talk about it before you do it. Talk about your plans and goals for money.

Appearance. Talk about your appearance, the way you dress. Tell each other what you like and what you don't like. Talk about the way you appear. Do you like that old bathrobe she was wearing today? If every time she puts something on and you go "yuck" on the inside, that's a sad thing to live with. Talk about it.

Children. I hope you talk about kids before you have them. If you already have them, I hope you are talking about how you are raising them. How are you training them? What kind of schooling are they getting? Do you know what your kids are doing in school? "Oh, I let the wife take care of that." How do you know she is doing it right? "Oh, I just trust her." Well that's good, but are you really trusting her or are you just lazy?

Spiritual life. Do you talk about prayer? Do you talk about verses in the Bible? Do you talk about the lessons you hear? Do you talk about what God is doing in your life? If you are not, then God is probably not doing too much in your life.

Activities. Do you talk about your activities? What do you like to do? What do you want to do? Some people say, "We don't do anything." You should start talking and doing some things, bowling or hiking or bike riding or something that you can do to have activities together. Do you talk about careers and business, do you talk about those things and know where you are headed and what you are doing? Those are basic areas you need to be communicating about regularly.

Love and submission are the two keys for a strong marriage. Ephesians 5 gives us the basis. The husband and wife first of all must submit to each other. If you will build your marriage around this concept, you will have success.

9
How to Prosper Financially

It is God's will for all people to prosper financially, and we are going to find out what the Word has to say about it. We are not concerned with tradition or what a denomination says. We want to know directly from the Word of God. In days gone by, to be a Christian you had to be associated with poverty. To be a minister you had to take vows of poverty. In the U.S.A. certain tax laws were established that had to do with benefits for Christians because they were committed to poverty. Now the church is starting to read the Bible and the government wants to change all the laws because the church is prospering. The Word of God has never changed, but people do. Some want to believe the Bible; some don't. Let's read what the Bible says, and then you make your decision.

Turn to Deuteronomy 8:18: "But thou shalt remember the Lord thy God: for it is he that giveth thee power to get wealth, that he may establish his covenant which he sware unto thy fathers, as it is this day." God committed Himself to give you the power to get wealth. He gave you the ability to get wealth, not to get poor. If you're going to take poverty vows, take them before the devil. The devil will teach you how to get poor, but God will teach you how to get wealth. Isn't that what it said? "Remember the Lord your God. It is He that giveth thee power to get wealth." God never gave anybody the ability to fail. He doesn't have failure, so He can't give it to you. What He does have is the wisdom and the knowledge to tell us how to win. He has given us the ability to win financially.

Now, you have to remember one thing about God that's a little different from people. God is not schizophrenic. God is not double-minded. God does not change in midstream. The Bible said in Malachi 3:6: "For I am the Lord, I change not . . ." Now, if God ever gave anybody the power to get wealth in the past, He'll still do it today; and, if He gives the power to get wealth, He won't give the power to get poor. He doesn't go back and forth. God doesn't change His mind like we do. We might decide to do one thing one day and then change our minds and do something else the next day, but God doesn't do that. He said, "Don't forget. Remember the Lord your God, for it is He that giveth thee the power to get wealth." It has always been that way. It always will be that way.

The reason He gives us the power is so that He may establish His covenant. His covenant is His Word. He wants to establish His Word in this earth. He wants the world to know His Word. And God knows that He is not going to get His Word established with a bunch of poverty-minded people. Poor people can't support missionaries. Poor people can't make TV broadcasts. Poor people can't build churches. The worst thing any preacher could ever do is teach people to be poor and then ask them for an offering. "Be poor. Don't have anything. Be a good Christian. Now you all come up here and give so we can send out this missionary." If you *do* have something to give, you are going to get confronted for having it.

If you apply the following verse to anything but money you are Biblically, scripturally wrong. II Corinthians 8:9: "For ye know the grace of our Lord Jesus Christ, that, though he was rich, yet for your sakes he became poor, that ye through his poverty might be rich." All of chapter 8 is about money. Paul starts out talking about the grace of the Lord that was on the churches. Verse 2 says: "How that in a great trial of affliction the abundance of their joy and deep poverty abounded to the riches of their liberality." They gave beyond their abilities. In other words, they were giving offerings, they were giving money, more than they could afford to give in the natural. And Paul says, "They have experienced the grace, and you all know the grace of our Lord. He became poor so that you could become rich." Jesus did that! Jesus lived in heaven, in the throne room of God. He was one with God, walking on the streets of gold, living in the most majestic, the most glorious, the most prosperous, the most extravagant place that the universe has ever known. I'm telling you if you get mad about extravagance, you are not going to like heaven. Everything about heaven is extravagant. One gate is a pearl. You think you're a hot rod because you've got one hanging around your neck. How would you like to walk up to somebody's door and find the door is just one big pearl? I'd like to see that oyster!

Jesus left all that. The Bible says He became poor. He came down here as a servant to help us. Why did He do it? So you could walk around poor? No. He became poor so that you might be rich. The Greek word rich, means "have an abundance financially."

III John 2 says: "Beloved, I wish above all things that thou mayest prosper and be in health, even as thy soul prospereth." He wants you to prosper even as your soul prospers. In other words, He wants you to be prosperous financially and be prosperous physically, which is to live in health even as your soul is prospering. God wants us to prosper in every realm of life. That's God's nature. God's nature is not one of lack.

Jesus never had any lack. When He walked around on the earth and 15,000 people showed up for lunch, He'd feed them all. He'd walk past a funeral, and He'd raise the dead. He didn't have any shortage of any kind. If He didn't have a boat, He'd just walk on the water. Jesus never went without. Some people say, "Yes, but in Matthew 8:20 it said: "And Jesus saith unto him, The foxes have holes, and the birds of the air have nests; but the Son of man hath not where to lay his head." All He is saying is, "I'm not taking time to lay down. I'm on the go. I'm traveling. If you want to come with me, you'd better be ready to move. I'm not going to let you rest and sit around on your rusty dusty." He was not saying He couldn't afford a house. He just didn't need one.

Did you ever read the book of Luke Chapter 8 where it says there were rich women who traveled with Jesus and took care of Him every place He went? That doesn't sound poverty stricken to me. They just traveled with Jesus and served Him and ministered to Him.

Prosperity is when we have enough for our own needs and desires as well as enough to give to others. You can apply that to any realm of life. Spiritual prosperity is when your spiritual needs are met and you have enough to help someone with their spiritual needs. Physical prosperity is when you are healthy and strong and can go over and help someone else become healthy and strong. Financial prosperity is when you have more than enough for your family and your desires and you can help someone else to prosper. When you can send finances to missionaries and meet their needs, pay their bills, that's prosperity. That doesn't necessarily mean you are a millionaire. It simply means you have more than enough.

The Bible says in II Corinthians 9:8: "And God is able to make all grace abound toward you; that ye, always having all sufficiency in all things, may abound to every good work." That's prosperity, and God will make you that way. The Amplified Bible says: "God is able to make all grace, every favor and earthly blessing come to you in abundance, so that you may always and under all circumstances and whatever the need, be self sufficient possessing enough to require no aid or support and furnished in abundance for every good work and charitable donation." That's prosperity. You have more than enough for any need that arises. You have more than enough for any situation that comes up, and God is able to place you in that position, enough for yourself and your family and to help those around you. If you are not prospering there is no way that you can help the poor or help to spread the gospel. There is no way. If you don't have it, how are you going to help someone else to get it? If you and I are both in the hole, are you going to pull me out? No. You have to get out of the hole first. *Then* you can help me.

What is the first thing you need to do to help the poor? Don't be one of them. Even a poverty-minded person can figure that out. See, some preachers think they are really spiritual when they say, "Well, bless God, we're going to serve the Lord. We're going to count the cost, and I'll tell you what; we're going to have to live on next to nothing if we want to really get close to the Lord. We are going to have to get away from all these luxuries and barely get by." Well, if you're going to barely get by, how are you going to help the poor? The fact is, since Jesus told His people to help the poor, He obviously didn't plan on you being one of the poor. If He planned on you being one of them, He would have said, "Go help yourself." But He didn't. He planned for you to prosper so you could help the poor.

God has always desired for His people to have enough to bless others. Prosperity is a part of our covenant with God. Poverty is a part of the curse. From the day God created man and began to relate to him on this earth it has always been the same.

Those who follow God walked in prosperity and those who rebelled against God were under a curse of poverty. It has never changed. It started with Adam in the book of Genesis and the garden of Eden. It went right on through to Moses, Abraham, Isaac, Jacob, Joseph, David, Solomon, every person that ever was involved with the Old Covenant. Those who walked with God were prosperous and had more than enough. Those who were against God were poor. It has never changed, and it never will change.

Somebody who supposedly was a great preacher said, "In the Old Covenant when you walked with God you were blessed financially, but in the New Covenant when you walk with God you suffer in poverty." Of course, that preacher forgot to mention that he only flies in private jet airplanes. He lives on a mountain which he owns with guards all around it. He has a little mansion built back into the hills where no one can get to him. He drops in by helicopter to come home. He forgot to mention that part, you know, but, yes, amen, he believes in poverty. Now, I think he should have his mountain. I think he should have his jet and his helicopter, but I think he should tell the people that they could have it too if they want it. The sin is not him having it. The sin is in having it and then telling everybody that he doesn't believe in the prosperity that brought it.

I saw this one preacher on TV. The interviewer asked, "Well, what's your salary?" He replied, "Oh, I just have a small salary." "But you live like a millionaire. You're wearing that Rolex watch." "Oh, somebody gave that to me. I really don't know how much it's worth. They probably got it wholesale." "Well, doesn't your wife wear a mink coat?" "Well, I think somebody gave her a mink coat. I guess it was a mink. I'm really not sure." Now, he knows his wife is wearing a mink coat, and he knows what his watch is worth, too. He knows exactly how much he is making and what he has, but, you see, he's lying to the people.

His wife went out and bought a $12,000 desk. People got mad about that. Here's what someone said, "Is it true that your wife bought a big desk?" He replied, "Well, now, you know, we got a special bargain basement price." You know what he should say? "That's right! And if they made a $15,000 one I'd like to get that one, too." And the same is true of his watch: "That's right. This is the best in the world. If they make one better, I'd like to get it." About the mink coat, he should say, "She has five mink coats, because God has designed for me to get wealth. I know the grace of our Lord Jesus. He became poor so that I could be rich. If you journalists would follow God, you would prosper, too." But see, lying and trying to cover it up and hide it, that's wrong. Prosperity is part of our covenant with God.

We need to start telling the world, "You bet we're prospering. If you'd serve God you would prosper, too. If you don't serve God you are under a curse and the devil will keep you poor and miserable. Now make your own choice, but I am going to go with God." If we start talking that way, the world will come on into the church.

One day I was being interviewed for TV. The guy walked around all day with me. He said, "I see you drive a Cadillac." I said, "Yes. Praise the Lord!" "What do people think about that?" I said, "I don't care." He said, "Well, you're supposed to be a pastor. People might not like it." I said, "If I'm poor, people are going to think church doesn't work. People don't want to be poor. If I'm rich, people are going to think I'm just in it for the money. So I'm just going to do what I want to do." That part of the interview got on TV, too!

I pulled into a gas station one day. My license plate at that time was "CFC" for "Christian Faith Center." There was a young guy pumping gas and he said, "Are you the CFC?" I said, "That's me. That's Christian Faith Center." He said, "You're so young. How come you're driving a Cadillac?" I said, "I serve Jesus." He said, "What?" I said, "I serve Jesus, and He blesses me." He said, "I guess He does!" I witnessed to that man about the covenant I have with my God. If I pulled up there in my old jalopy, what kind of testimony would that be? "Serve God, and He'll get you a jalopy." That isn't a testimony! The Bible said the New Covenant is built on better promises. Well, if the Old Covenant says, "God gives you power to get wealth," He's doing something even better today. Poverty is not better than wealth. It's like one brother said, "I've been poor, and I've been rich. Rich is better."

I'm not going to take the time to go over Deuteronomy 28, but read the first 15 verses. It tells you what will happen to you if you obey God. Let me just paraphrase it a little bit. "If you hearken diligently unto the voice of the Lord your God to observe to do according to all that is written in His commandments, all these blessings will come upon you. You will be blessed in the city, blessed in the field. Your bank account will be blessed. Your house will be blessed. Your children will be blessed your spouse will be blessed. Your business will be blessed. Your nation will be blessed. Everything you set your hand to do will be blessed." Verse 15 says: "But if you choose not to hearken unto the voice of the Lord your God, if you do not obey the voice of the Lord your God, all these curses will come on you. Your house will be cursed. Your children will be cursed. Your bank account will be cursed. Your savings account will be cursed. Everything you do will be cursed, and you will be sick, and you will be poor."

Look at Galations 3:13,14: "Christ hath redeemed us from the curse of the law, being made a curse for us: for it is written, Cursed is every one that hangeth on a tree: That the blessing of Abraham might come on the Gentiles through Jesus Christ; that we might receive the promise of the Spirit through faith." What did Jesus die for? So you wouldn't have to be under the curse. What was the curse? Spiritual death is part of it. Sickness and disease is part of it. Poverty is part of it. Those three things sum up the curse. Why did Jesus die? So you wouldn't have spiritual death, sickness, or poverty, but, instead, you would be spiritually alive and healthy and prosperous, so you would have the blessing of Abraham. The Bible said that he was very rich in silver and gold and cattle. (I'll take the

silver and gold. You can have the cattle.) You can
read about that in Genesis 12:1-3 and Genesis 13:2.
When you read it, you will find out how Abraham
was blessed, and the Bible says Jesus came so *you*
could have the same blessing.

God's will is that all people prosper. He said, "I
pray above all things that you would prosper." And
yet you know that God's will does not happen automatically. It's God's will that all people get born
again, but we know that not everyone will be born
again. It's God's will for all people to be healthy,
and yet we know not everybody will receive divine
health. It's God's will that everybody be full of joy.
Yet in the Christian world not everybody will walk
in joy. There are those who just choose not to do it.
Even though it is God's will, they refuse it. They do
not accept it. They do not agree with it. So,
although it is God's will for you to prosper, you are
going to have to do things God's way in order to
receive God's will, and God's prosperity is always
based on the seed-sowing principle.

Luke 6:38 is probably the verse that most clearly
describes the seed-sowing principle. In this chapter
Jesus is speaking about many things. He speaks
about love, mercy, and forgiveness, but He gives the
principle for all these things in verse 38: "Give, and
it shall be given unto you; good measure, pressed
down, and shaken together, and running over, shall
men give into your bosom. For with the same measure that ye mete withal it shall be measured to you
again." This same principle is repeated in II Corinthians 9, in Galations 6, and in the Old Testament
in many places, but the point is: Whatever you give

decides what you will receive. If you give mercy, you will receive mercy. If you give forgiveness, you will receive forgiveness. If you give hostility, you will receive hostility. If you will give finances, you will receive finances. You see, it is a seed-sowing principle. If you plant a seed, you will get a harvest. If you plant cotton, you will get cotton. If you don't plant anything, you will get nothing, not a thing. "I don't understand why God never blesses me." "Well, do you give your tithes?" "No, I can't afford it." "Well, that's why. You're not sowing any seeds, so you're not reaping a harvest."

What would the farmer do if he went out to his fields and said, "I can't understand why you're not growing any cotton. What's wrong with you, field? Are you mad at me?" His neighbor would come over to the fence and say, "Hey, brother, did you sow cotton seed?" "No, I can't afford it. I'm waiting for my harvest to come up, and then I'll go and get some." You're not going to get a crop until you plant some seed. When you plant the seed, then you get the crop. And everybody has been given seed to plant.

"Give and it shall be given unto you," and He'll increase what you give. See, you plant one seed of corn, but you don't just get one seed of corn back. You get many seeds of corn back. If you plant one little cotton seed, you're not going to get just one piece of cotton. You get a whole bush full of cotton. "Give and it shall be given unto you, good measure, pressed down, shaken together and running over." Notice the last phrase, "For with the same measure that you mete withal it shall be measured to you again."

When we give willingly and cheerfully, God blesses our giving, and brings it back to us in abundance. But, so often, people think this is a get rich quick plan, and they give with a teaspoon and expect to receive with a dump truck. "I want a thousand dollars for this nickel." Now, if a teaspoon is *really* all you have to give, that's another story, and God will bless you and cause you to have more. But, if you give with a teaspoon when you should be giving with a bucket, God will give it back to you with whatever you gave it to Him. You scoop to Him with teaspoons, and He'll scoop back with teaspoons. If you plant an acre what are you going to reap? One acre. Now the average farmer is not going to make a whole lot of money on one acre. That's why farmers have 200, 300, 500, 1000 acres. They want big harvests; so they have to plant big fields. If you're like me and you want a big harvest, you are going to have to get to planting a lot of seed. Just tipping God your little $5 every month is not going to get you a big harvest. Over half of the church doesn't tithe, and then people wonder why they have financial problems.

People rebel against God. They think they are smarter. They think, "Well you don't understand my situation." Don't base your life on your situation. Base your life on the Word of God. God said, "Give and it shall be given unto you." "Well, if I get something I'll give something." You might as well forget it. God's prosperity is always based on the seed-sowing principle. If a person says, "I don't believe in that prosperity stuff," I know right away that person is selfish. It is impossible to give without God blessing you. If you don't believe in prosperity, I know you are selfish.

Do you know that most preachers don't tithe? I think it is only about 2% of the preachers in the whole country of all denominations and affiliations tithe. That will tell you why most churches are poor. At Christian Faith Center, the tithing starts with the pastor and the pastoral staff. I make sure the staff, including myself, is giving over their tithes. I might ask the staff sometimes to give 20%. I don't force them. I don't make them. They do it because they want to. It starts with the staff and then goes on to the church body. The giving in our church is a lot better than most places, and yet over half of the people are still missing out on the blessing. They are missing out. They think they are real smart: "Well, you aren't going to get my money." You aren't hurting me, but you are robbing yourself and robbing God. Without sowing seed there is no harvest. Look at II Corinthians 9:6: "But this I say, He which soweth sparingly shall reap also sparingly; and he which soweth bountifully shall reap also bountifully."

If your life is very sparse, you now know why. If your life is very sparse right now, that's all you have been sowing. Again, this is in any area. "I don't have any friends." Well, what you are telling me is that you are not friendly. Friendly people have lots of friends. When you give friendship, you receive friendship. "Well, I don't have anybody I am close to." Well, you're not putting yourself out to be close. See, you're waiting for other people to do it, but the Bible says *you* do it and then you will receive. I'm not saying this to be mean. That's just the way life is. You just can't get around the seed-sowing principle.

You have to make a decision in your heart to give. The feeling is not going to come on you. A lot of times we say in the church, "Well, give what you are led," and people don't give anything because they are waiting for the giving feeling and there "ain't no giving feeling." *You purpose it in your heart.* You make a decision. Now there are times when the Holy Spirit will specifically lead people and direct them in special cases. We have had special offerings where I believe the Holy Spirit was specifically leading people. But Paul said, "Purpose in your heart." Make a decision about what you are going to give.

Wendy and I sit down and make a decision: "How much of our income are we going to give before we figure out all the rest of the bills?" We do this before we figure out if we are going to get a raise that year or what the other bills are going to be. Before we figure whether we are going to buy a car, whether we are going to buy a new oven or whatever else, we first decide on how much we are going to give. And every couple of months we increase it. If we are going to give 20 or 30 percent to the church, then we are going to give another 10% to other ministries: radio ministers, people who are holding seminars and preaching around the country, and things like that. *And* we are going to give a certain amount of our money to poor people who cannot afford to take care of their own needs. Then we get all the other bills and all the other desires of our heart and we decide how are we going to be able to do this and do that. That's why we have an abundance, not because I am a preacher. There are a whole bunch of folks who are preachers who are as poor as poor can be. But, see, we decide to sow bountifully, and when we sow bountifully we reap bountifully.

You make the decision to give or not to give. If you don't make a decision to give, it won't happen. It isn't real to say, "As soon as I get a whole bunch, I'll be a giver." If you are not faithful over little, you will never be faithful over much. If you can't give $10 off that $100 check, there is no way you are going to give $100 off that $1,000 check. II Corinthians 9:7 says: "Every man according as he purposeth in his heart, so let him give; not grudgingly, or of necessity: for God loveth a cheerful giver." Notice it says, "Not grudgingly." You won't get a return if you give grudgingly. He said to do it cheerfully. "God loveth a cheerful giver." When you are happy about giving, then you will be happy about receiving.

God knows your heart. You can't deceive Him. Galations 6:7-9 says: "Be not deceived; God is not mocked: for whatsoever a man soweth, that shall he also reap. For he that soweth to his flesh shall of the flesh reap corruption." You see, people are always interested in getting their houses paid and getting their cars and getting this and getting that. I know some people who say, "We would like to tithe, Brother Treat, but we haven't paid off our TV yet." Well, that is just sowing to the flesh. "Well, I'd like to tithe, Brother Treat, but I want to get a new car.

I've had the same car for the last five years. Now, don't you think God wants me to have a new car?" Sure He does, but don't be deceived. You can't play games with God. "For he that soweth to his flesh shall of the flesh reap corruption; but he that soweth to the Spirit shall of the Spirit reap life everlasting. And let us not be weary in well doing: for in due season we shall reap, if we faint not." In other words, if we don't quit sowing the seed, we will reap. A lot of people sow one time and then they wait to see if it's going to come back. "I put $10 in. I'm waiting for my hundred. As soon as I get it, I'll sow a little more." See, the farmer just keeps sowing seed every season. He never quits, because the day he does he will stop reaping.

Tithing is the basis for all giving and receiving. If you do not tithe you are not in God's prosperity plan. If you are coming to church and just tipping God, that's all right, but if you want to get in His financial plan you have to tithe. That means give a tenth of what you earn on a weekly basis. If your salary is $50 a week, then you bring $5 into the storehouse, the church. If you are making $100 a week, you bring in $10.

You might ask, "Well is that before taxes or after taxes?" Taxes are a part of your income. You live in this country. You drive on this country's roads. The country's police are looking after you. That's a part of your income. If you don't want to pay taxes, leave the country. I'll send you where they don't have any taxes. Of course, you can't go to church there either or even read the Bible. You can't have your own car, either. There you just do what they tell you to do. If you are living here, you are going to pay taxes. That's a part of your income.

Tithing is when we give a tenth of our income to the church where we are getting fed. Now, some people go to church where they aren't being fed, and the Bible said, "Don't give your money to a dead work." That's in Deuteronomy 26. I know some people who are going to dead churches where nobody has been born again in months and nobody talks in tongues. In fact the preacher says, "You are going to talk in tongues over my dead body." They haven't sent out missionaries. They haven't gotten anybody baptized in the Holy Ghost. They haven't had a healing service in who knows how long, and yet the people keep giving their money to those dead works. Then they come to Christian Faith Center to get fed! "Well, we have a home church, Brother Treat. We come over here to get fed."

What do you suppose would happen if I went down tonight to my favorite restaurant and the maitre d' said, "Well, good evening, Mr. Treat. How many are in your party?" "Hello. There will be four of us tonight." He takes us down to a nice, beautiful window seat, and I look out over the beautiful lights and the Northwest scenery. I have my nice halibut or whatever I desire. I have my ice tea and have my dessert (health food, you know), and I say, "Thank you, sir. That will be all." Then I get up and walk out. "Sir, uh, Mr. Treat, aren't you forgetting something?" "No, I decided I'm going to go across the street and pay at Denny's. I have my home restaurant. I'm just here to get fed." Now, do you suppose I am going to make it to the door? No way!

They are going to have the security police on me like white on rice. You pay where you get fed.

Now, let's take a look at another story. I go into the restaurant. I sit down, and the waiter comes and says, "Mr. Treat, I am sorry, but the kitchen is completely out of food. We don't have any food here. All we have is water. You can sit in the chair if you'd like, but there is no food." So I say, "Okay, let me sit here for a few minutes and decide what I am going to do." So I sit there and chat with my friends for a few minutes, and then I get up to leave, and he brings me a bill. I say, "What's this?" He says, "Usually when you come in here you like halibut and iced tea and dessert, and that comes to $25.95. Here's the bill." "But I didn't get any food. I didn't eat!" He says, "Yes, but you know how it is. When you come, you have to pay the bill." Now, you know I am not going to go for that. I am not going to pay to sit in a restaurant that doesn't have any food! So what are some of you doing sitting in a church where you aren't getting fed and paying a bill for nothing?

So now you say, "Okay, I've been out of God's will. I want to change. What do I do?" Look at Malachi 3:8: "Will a man rob God? Yet ye have robbed me. But ye say, Wherein have we robbed thee? In tithes and offerings." The first thing to do is get your money in line with God's Word. Why? If you will get your money in line, you will get your whole life in line because your money is your blood, sweat, and tears. See, giving is not just some light, flippant thing. If you refuse to give your money, what you are saying is, "Lord, you don't have control over my life. I refuse to submit to you. I'm not going to give to you. I'm going to keep it." And Jesus said in Matthew 10:39: "If you keep your life you will lose it, but if you give your life you will save it." God said in verse 9 of Malachi 3: "Ye are cursed with a curse: for ye have robbed me, even this whole nation."

Many times I've heard people say, "Brother Treat, just as soon as we have a little bit of money in the savings account, what do you suppose happened? The car broke down. The pipes broke. We had to do some work on the house. We spent all of our money." Well, what do you suppose that is caused from? The devourer. As soon as you've got something to devour, he's going to eat it up. You get a little bit ahead, and the devourer now has something to devour. As long as you don't have any food in the house, mice don't hang around. You get a little food in there and the mouse is going to come in and eat it if he can. You must take the proper steps to keep him out. If you have not taken the proper steps to keep the devourer away, he is going to come in and wipe you out. But God tells you how to get rid of him in verse 10: "Bring ye all the tithes into the storehouse..."

Notice he says, "Bring ye *all*." He didn't say leave a little bit here and a little bit there and spread it all over the nation. He said to bring all the tithes into one place, the storehouse, not storehouses. Your tithe goes to the local church where you are being fed.

If you say, "I go wherever the Spirit leads me," and you are attending more than one church, then you are in the flesh, because the Spirit won't lead you to more than one church. You are supposed to be in a place where you can be a part. Church hoppers are out of the will of God. He wants His children to be members of a church body. He has a place for each of us. He says to bring your tithes, the whole tenth, into the storehouse, singular, and He goes on to say, "that there may be meat in mine house," meaning, "so the storehouse can send the Word out to feed people, to feed the sheep." Jesus said, "Feed my sheep." That's why we have TV and radio and missionaries and books and tapes and Bibles, to feed the sheep. I'll tell you: come around here, and you are going to get some meat. Whenever you come, any day, any hour, you are going to be fed. That's why people bring their tithes here. And that's how it should be in your church. "Prove me now herewith, saith the Lord of hosts, if I will not open you the windows of heaven, and pour you out a blessing, that there shall not be room enough to receive it."

This is the only place in the Bible where God says, "Prove it." You remember when you were a little kid in school and you would smart off to somebody and say, "Oh, I could come over there and knock your lights out," and the other one said, "Prove it," and then all of a sudden you heard mom call, to your great relief! "Well, I've got to go now." See, it's one thing to talk, and it's another thing to prove it. God said, "I am going to open you the windows of heaven, and I can prove it. Put me to the test. I'll show you that it is true." Now look at verses 11 & 12: "And I will rebuke the devourer for your sakes, and he shall not destroy the fruits of your ground; neither shall your vine cast her fruit before the time in the field, saith the Lord of hosts. And all nations shall call you blessed: for ye shall be a delightsome land, saith the Lord of hosts." Tithes and offerings will put you in that place. "Well, Brother Treat, I'm not going for that." Well, then stay the way you are and don't complain.

Look at Proverbs 3:9: "Honor the Lord with thy substance, and with the first fruits of all thine increase." Do you know what that means? The first fruit is the very first thing that you receive. You see, what most people do with their tithing and their offering is they get their check, pay all their bills, and if they have anything left they tip God. God will not accept your doggy bags. The Lord stressed this on me one day and it kind of shook me, but it is the truth. I'm not going to go to a restaurant and then bring someone I love my leftovers to eat for dinner. "It was a really great meal, Wendy. Here's your portion in the doggy bag. Aren't I great to think about you?" Let me tell you, I'd be in a heap of trouble! Well, God doesn't want your doggy bags either. That's why so many of you are under the curse and your finances are terrible, and you're not going to get out of it because you are taking God your little doggy bags. He said, "Bring me the first-fruits." When you do, God will honor you.

We are to make sure that money doesn't control us. Turn to Matthew 6:33: "But seek ye first the kingdom of God, and his righteousness; and all these things shall be added unto you." Seek first the kingdom. We are to have money; it is not to have us. The only way to guard against the love of money is to be a giver. Did you know you can be flat broke and be in love with money? Not just rich folks have the love of money. A lot of poor folks have the love of money, too. The only way you can know that you are not involved with the love of money is if you are a giver. The basic reason some of you don't tithe is because you are selfish and you love money. "Oh, Brother Treat, you can say that because you have a lot of money." I started tithing when I was on welfare. I got a welfare check for $140 a month, and the tithe went to the Lord. I gave offerings out of my welfare check, too. The basic reason people don't give, don't tithe, is that they are selfish and they love money. If you will renew your mind to God's Word, He'll give you more money than you ever dreamed of. He'll open you the windows of heaven and pour you out a blessing. He will rebuke the devourer, but you are going to have to do it *His* way.

10
Leadership in the Church

God, through His Word, has given clear instruction to the church as to how it is to be lead and governed. When God's plan is followed, there will be success. When we do our own thing, it will eventually lead to failure. Any organization that is moving forward, whether it be a business, a large or small corporation, a city, or a nation, must have leadership. The church is no different. In order for the church to progress and grow and to function effectively, it must have leadership.

Before we take a look at the Biblical structure for church leadership, I want to show you some basics about traditional patterns that denominations have established.

Episcopalian Church Government

In this plan, bishops have authority over the pastors and local churches. It is found in Roman Catholic, Anglican, Episcopalian, Methodist, and other churches. The title "Bishop" comes from the Greek word "Episkopos" which means "overseer or superintendent." To use the Roman Catholic church as an example: The roles of authority start with the

Pope. Under him is the cardinal bishop, the archbishop, the bishop. Under the bishop is the local bishop, and at the bottom is the pastor or priest. Each level of bishop has the authority to tell the local pastor how to lead the flock. We will see in scripture that this disagrees with God's plan for church leadership.

Presbyterian Church Government

This form of leadership establishes a group of "elders" in charge of church functions. The Greek word "presbiteros" is translated "presbytery" in the New Testament, and it means "elder." This committee type leadership is found in Presbyterian, Holiness, and many nondenominational churches. The elders vote to decide church direction, and the pastor is then told what to do accordingly. If a new pastor is desired, the elders or presbyters make the choices concerning a new pastor. As we study the role of a pastor, we will find much conflict with scripture concerning this form of government.

Congregational Church Government

In this pattern, it is obvious the whole congregation leads itself. It is much like the democratic form of government in the U.S. In fact, this form of church organization came into being around the beginning of the United States. Churches operating under this kind of leadership include the Assemblies of God, the Baptists, Churches of Christ, and the Congregationalists. In this case, a vote is taken from the congregation on issues regarding church direction, and the pastor is directed to carry out that vote. It's kind of like the body telling the head what to do.

Biblical Church Government

While each of the traditional forms of government have strengths, the overall effectiveness of leadership is stifled, and God's will for the church is generally missed. As I said before, anytime man comes up with a plan other than God's, you will eventually see failure. Ephesians 1:22,23 says: "And hath put all things under his feet, and gave him to be the head over all things to the church, which is his body, the fulness of him that filleth all in all."

Jesus is the builder of the church. He is the head of the body and in charge of all church leadership. He is to decide what happens, when it happens, how it happens, and who is to lead it. Jesus said in Matthew 16:18: "And I say also unto thee, That thou art Peter, and upon this rock I will build my church; and the gates of hell shall not prevail against it." The church that is established by God and led by the person Jesus chooses is built on a solid foundation. The gates of hell and all of Satan's forces cannot stand against the church that is established on the Word of God and led according to the Word of God. The plan for church leadership that God has given us is strong, powerful, and very effective if we will only follow it. In I Corinthians 12:28 we read: "And God hath set some in the church, first apostles, secondarily prophets, thirdly teachers, after that miracles, then gifts of healings, helps, governments, diversities of tongues."

God has set some in the church. Notice it didn't say that some are voted in or promoted into those positions. It simply and clearly says, "God has set some in the church." In Ephesians 4:11 it goes on to tell us about the leaders God the Father and Jesus the Son have put into the church. "And he gave some, apostles; and some, prophets; and some, evangelists; and some, pastors and teachers."

Pastors and teachers are included in the list of five leaders Jesus put into the church. They are part of the leadership structure God established. They weren't meant to be the silent partner in the church. They are placed there by God to lead the church, the body of Christ.

We've read that God sets some in the church, and we've read that Jesus is head over the church; therefore, the ones who are called or set in the church are responsible to the one who called them. Jesus calls the pastors and puts them in the church, so the pastors are under the authority of and are responsible to Jesus. That's how God designed the church to operate.

If we look at some of the traditional church leadership in light of what we have just read, this is what we find. If a group of elders or a bishop or the congregation puts in a pastor, then the pastor is responsible to them and not to Jesus. We have *men* calling the pastors, so the pastors are responsible to men. In Biblical church government, you have God calling the pastors, and the pastors are responsible to God.

Pastor

"Pastor" means "shepherd." The pastor is the shepherd of the flock of God known as the church. He is responsible to feed the flock. Peter said to the elders, who were pastors, in I Peter 5:1-4: "The elders which are among you I exhort, who am also an elder, and a witness of the sufferings of Christ, and also a partaker of the glory that shall be revealed: Feed the flock of God which is among you, taking the oversight thereof, not by constraint, but willingly; not for filthy lucre, but of a ready mind; Neither as being lords over God's heritage, but being ensamples to the flock. And when the chief Shepherd shall appear, ye shall receive a crown of glory that fadeth not away."

The pastor's responsibility is to feed the congregation the Word of God so they will grow up in Christ. He is not to be visiting every sick person or new member who comes into the church. James 5:14 says: "Is any sick among you? let him call for the elders of the church; and let them pray over him, anointing him with oil in the name of the Lord." The pastor is not to be the church bookkeeper or janitor. He is to feed the flock, the congregation. Ephesians 4:11-15 says: "And he gave some, apostles; and some, prophets; and some, evangelists; and some, pastors and teachers; for the perfecting of the saints, for the work of the ministry, for the edifying of the body of Christ: Till we all come in the unity of the faith, and of the knowledge of the Son of God, unto a perfect man, unto the measure of the stature of the fullness of Christ: That we henceforth be no more children, tossed to and fro, and carried about with every wind of doctrine, by the sleight of men, and cunning craftiness, whereby they lie in wait to deceive; But speaking the truth in love, may grow up into him in all things, which is the head, even Christ."

The pastor is not to do all the work of the ministry, but he is to perfect or equip the saints to do it. There is no way a pastor can do all the work in the kingdom of God, but he can prepare the congregation to do it. A good pastor is a trainer or coach who leads all the church people to do God's work. As Jesus is the head of the universal church, so the pastor is the head of the local church. When the body follows the head, you have good results; but, when the body tries to tell the head what to do, you have failure. Hebrews 13:17 says, "Obey them that have the rule over you, and submit yourselves: for they watch for your souls, as they that must give account, that they may do it with joy, and not with grief: for that is unprofitable for you."

The Bible also tells us what a pastor's salary should be like. I Timothy 5:17,18: "Let the elders that rule well be counted worthy of double honor, especially they who labor in the word and doctrine. For the scripture saith, Thou shalt not muzzle the ox that treadeth out the corn. And the laborer is worthy of his reward." "Double honor" literally means "double remuneration." According to this verse the pastors or head elders who teach the flock should be paid double what other church leaders are. The Bible never speaks of pastors or anyone else taking poverty vows or living in lack to be spiritual. Paul said in II Corinthians 8:9: "For ye know the grace of our Lord Jesus Christ, that, though he was rich, yet for your sakes he became poor, that ye through his poverty might be rich."

Elders

Where do elders fit into this plan? I Timothy 3:1 says: "This is a true saying, If a man desire the office of a bishop, he desireth a good work." Notice the office of an elder can be desired and aspired to. A pastor is called by God, but the elders are chosen by the pastor. Acts 14:23: "And when they had ordained them elders in every church, and had prayed with fasting, they commended them to the Lord, on whom they believed." The pastor could be called the head elder, and the men or women who are chosen to be elders act as his advisors. Elders are to help the pastor with the spiritual oversight of the church. Acts 20:28 says: "Take heed therefore unto yourselves, and to all the flock, over the which the Holy Ghost hath made you overseers, to feed the church of God, which he hath purchased with his own blood." They are not just money counters or business consultants. They are to be spiritual aids to the pastor's office. Many times the elders are influential men because of money or position but are in no way spiritual leaders. This is contrary to Biblical church leadership. I Timothy 3:1-7 gives us the qualifications for an elder: "This is a true saying, If a man desire the office of a bishop, he desireth a good work. A bishop then must be blameless, the husband of one wife, vigilant, sober, of good behavior, given to hospitality, apt to teach; Not given to wine, no striker, not greedy of filthy lucre; but patient, not a brawler, not covetous; One that ruleth well his own house, having his children in subjection with all gravity; (For if a man know not how to rule his own house, how shall he take care of the church of God?) Not a novice, lest being lifted up with pride he fall into the condemnation of the devil. Moreover he must have a good report of them which are without; lest he fall into reproach and the snare of the devil."

In Titus 2:1-3 we find that women can be in the position of elder or elderess: "But speak thou the things which become sound doctrine: That the aged men be sober, grave, temperate, sound in faith, in charity, in patience. The aged women likewise, that they be in behavior as becometh holiness, not false accusers, not given to much wine, teachers of good things." In verse 3, the words "aged women" is actually the Greek word "presuteros" in the female gender. So we have the elderess, and she is to teach good things. The women are not to usurp authority over the men in leadership, but it is obvious that women are to be part of church leadership. Here are a few scriptures showing the leadership positions established for women in the church. Acts 2:17,18: "And it shall come to pass in the last days, saith God, I will pour out of my Spirit upon all flesh: and your sons and your daughters shall prophesy, and your young men shall see visions, and your old men shall dream dreams: And on my servants and on my handmaidens I will pour out in those days of my Spirit; and they shall prophesy." Romans 16:1: "I commend unto you Phebe our sister, which is a servant of the church which is at Cenchrea." Romans 16:3-5: "Greet Priscilla and Aquila my helpers in Christ Jesus: Who have for my life laid down their own necks: unto whom not only I give thanks, but also all the churches of the Gentiles.

Likewise greet the church that is in their house. Salute my well beloved Epaenetus, who is the first fruits of Achaia unto Christ." Galations 3:28: "There is neither Jew nor Greek, there is neither bond nor free, there is neither male nor female: for ye are all one in Christ Jesus."

Any church that does not utilize the leadership abilities of its women is unscriptural and foolish in this regard. A modern day example of women in leadership can be seen at the largest church in the world where Paul Yonggi Cho has used women to head over two-thirds of his ministry outreach. With several hundred thousand members in 1985, it's obvious God's blessing is upon that church and its leadership.

Deacons

The word "deacon" or "diakonos" in the Greek literally means "servant" or "minister." In many churches the deacons control all areas of the ministry, including the pastor, but let's look at their position based on scripture. Acts 6:1-7 says: "And in those days, when the number of the disciples was multiplied, there arose a murmuring of the Grecians against the Hebrews, because their widows were neglected in the daily ministration. Then the twelve called the multitude of the disciples unto them, and said, It is not reason that we should leave the word of God, and serve tables. Wherefore, brethren, look ye out among you seven men of honest report, full of the Holy Ghost and wisdom, whom we may appoint over this business. But we will give ourselves continually to prayer, and to the ministry of the word. And the saying pleased the whole multitude: and they chose Stephen, a man full of faith and of the Holy Ghost, and Philip, and Prochorus, and Nicanor, and Timon, and Parmenas, and Nicolas a proselyte of Antioch: Whom they set before the apostles: and when they had prayed, they laid their hands on them. And the word of God increased; and the number of the disciples multiplied in Jerusalem greatly; and a great company of the priests were obedient to the faith."

These seven men were the first deacons. They were servants of the people, helpers to the apostles. Their job started as waiting on tables or distributing food to the widows. Some of them (like Philip) later went into other ministries. Deacons are to be helpers in the administrative functions of church operations. They handle parking lots, ushering, offerings, etc.

The qualifications for a deacon are listed in I Timothy 3:8-13: "Likewise must the deacons be grave, not double-tongued, not given to much wine, not greedy of filthy lucre; holding the mystery of the faith in a pure conscience. And let these also first be proved; then let them use the office of a deacon, being found blameless. Even so must their wives be grave, not slanderers, sober, faithful in all things. Let the deacons be the husbands of one wife, ruling their children and their own houses well. For they that have used the office of a deacon well purchase to themselves a good degree, and great boldness in the faith which is in Christ Jesus."

Conclusion

When all the church leaders: pastors, elders, and deacons, function as the Word of God says, the church will prosper and grow. Acts 6:7 says: "And the word of God increased; and the number of the disciples multiplied in Jerusalem greatly; and a great company of the priests were obedient to the faith." This happened when church government was put in order. I know God wants to do the same thing today as He did in the early days of the church. When we obey His Word, it will come to pass.

11
The Last Days

The "End Times" is one area which has been talked about, explained, debated, and presumed upon for centuries, not all of which has been based on the Word of God. As we have listened to all these thoughts and ideas, we have formed opinions about the end times, but we have not necessarily taken the time to find out if our ideas and opinions line up with the Word of God.

Most of the time when we have trouble understanding or learning something, it's because we already have a picture in our minds of how it is supposed to be. We miss what the Word of God says. If we have an opinion already in mind, we won't hear what someone else is saying about it. We think we already know it all. So I encourage you to look at these scriptures with an open mind. Put aside your thoughts and ideas and seek after God's Word. Let's see what God's Word says about the end times.

When Jesus returns, there will be a literal catching up of the church (rapture) to meet the Lord in the air. I put the word rapture in parentheses because that term is not used in the Bible. Different

146

religious groups will challenge you and say, "Did you know that the rapture is not in the Bible?" If you haven't studied it a whole lot, you'll say, "Well, yes, it is." And they'll say, "No it's not. Look right here in this concordance and see if you can find the word 'rapture.' " Many Christian people have fallen to doctrines of devils or to cultist teachings because they didn't realize that someone just played a word game on them. It's true the *word* "rapture" is not in the Bible, but we do find the *concept* of rapture in the Bible. It is called a "catching up" or a "catching away." I want to make you aware of this so you won't get caught in that little word game if someone tries to trick you.

Now turn to I Thessalonians 4:14: "For if we believe that Jesus died and rose again, even so them also which sleep in Jesus will God bring with him." There is a whole mouthful in that verse, so follow along closely. First of all, we believe that Jesus died and rose again. Those who have already died being Christians, or in Jesus, God will bring with Him. The particular church Paul is talking to here had the concept that if you died before Jesus returned you missed out on heaven. See, the devil comes to tell anybody *anything* to try to discourage and scare them and put them into condemnation, but Paul came along and straightened them out on what actually will happen in the end times. He said, "Those who sleep in Jesus, or died being Christians, God will send with Jesus when He returns." Well, that tells us two things: First of all, that Jesus is going to be coming back; and, secondly, those who have already died are going to be with Him. Verse 15: "For this we say unto you by the word of the Lord, that we which are alive and remain unto the coming of the Lord shall not prevent them which are asleep."

There are some people who will be alive on the earth when the Lord comes. Paul said, "When He comes, those of us who are alive will not prevent, or we will not stop anyone else who has already died from also being with the Lord." Verses 16 and 17: "For the Lord himself shall descend from heaven with a shout, with the voice of the archangel, and with the trump of God: and the dead in Christ shall rise first: Then we which are alive and remain shall be caught up together with them in the clouds to meet the Lord in the air: and so shall we ever be with the Lord."

What's happening here? First Paul says those who are already dead will come with Jesus when He returns. Then he throws in something else: the dead in Christ will rise first. He said the dead in Christ will rise first, and yet he also said that they who are dead in Christ are going to come with Him. Now, how is that going to work? Well, just let me give you a picture of the rapture.

When Jesus returns, He is going to come to earth from heaven with a shout, with the voice of the archangel, and with the trump of God. He is going to have all the saints, all the Christian men and women who have died, with Him. But, remember, when they die and go to heaven two things happen, one, their bodies go in the ground; and, two, their spirits and souls go to heaven. So their spirits and souls are coming with the Lord when He returns to this earth, and their bodies will rise up before those who are still living rise up.

So Jesus is coming. The spirits and souls of all the Christians who have already died will be with Him. Their physical bodies will come up out of the ground and be recreated into their spiritual bodies. The spirits and souls will meet the spiritual bodies and will be together throughout eternity with Jesus. Those still living will be changed in the twinkling of an eye and receive recreated, glorified bodies. They will then meet the Lord in the air to also be with Him throughout eternity. That's what's going to take place at the rapture. It's going to be a catching up of the church, and it's going to be a receiving of glorified bodies.

The saints who are in heaven right now do not have glorified bodies. The only one we know has a glorified body right now is Jesus. We don't know about Elijah and Moses and Enoch. They might have their glorified bodies. Those guys are a little bit different. Enoch just walked with God and "was not." Elijah got sent up in a fiery chariot. Moses was up there on the Mount of Transfiguration with Jesus. Those three guys might already have their glorified bodies. I don't know. But the rest of the saints, in general, who have already died will receive their glorified bodies when their bodies are raised up at the rapture of the church. And then those who are still living will receive glorified bodies the moment they meet the Lord in the air. Look at verse 18: "Wherefore comfort one another with these words."

Did it say, "Scare one another to death with these

words?" No. It said "comfort one another." Any time you hear teaching that scares you, it is not from the Word of God. It's not God's teaching. He said, "Comfort one another with these words." Those verses are meant to give you comfort. Don't be afraid of physical death. As long as you are born again, there's nothing to fear.

The book of Revelation is the last book of the Bible. It gives the last picture God wanted the church to have of their stay on this earth. It also gives the picture of the year immediately preceding the church's departure. In Revelation 4:1-2, John is speaking, and he says: "After this I looked, and, behold, a door was opened in heaven: and the first voice which I heard was as it were of a trumpet talking with me; which said, Come up hither, and I will shew thee things which must be hereafter. And immediately I was in the spirit; and, behold, a throne was set in heaven, and one sat on the throne." Right there, John describes the rapture of the church. He said, "I heard that voice as a trumpet." Remember, we read back there that Jesus will return with the voice of the archangel, the trump of God. John said, "I heard that voice. It was like a trumpet talking to me. Immediately I was in the spirit." In a moment, in a twinkling of an eye, we'll be changed. John says it like this: "Immediately I was in the spirit." And then all of a sudden he realized he was in heaven in the throne room of God. That's what the rapture will be.

Now turn to Acts 1:9-11: "And when he had spoken these things, while they beheld, he was taken up; and a cloud received him out of their sight. And while they looked steadfastly toward heaven as he went up, behold, two men stood by them in white apparel; Which also said, Ye men of Galilee, why stand ye gazing up into heaven? this same Jesus, which is taken up from you into heaven, shall so come in like manner as ye have seen him go into heaven." When Jesus left the earth, they watched Him leave the earth. They watched Him go up as though He were on a heavenly elevator. While they were standing there looking up into the clouds, angels walked up and said, "What are you looking up into the clouds for? He's going to return the same way He left."

Some believe when we leave the earth during the rapture the sinners, those who are not born again, will see us leave as Jesus did. Unsaved husbands and wives will watch their mates leave. That would be the best altar call they could ever see. If that doesn't get them saved, they're pretty hard-hearted. Some believe that the sinners will see us rising out of our houses, rising out of our cars. If I had an airline service, I'd make sure not to put two Christians in the cockpit. If both of them get raptured, that plane is in trouble.

I really don't know if the world will see us leave or if we will just be gone. John said in Revelation 4, that immediately he was in the spirit. Once we do enter the spirit world, the natural world won't see us anymore. We're just gone in the twinkling of an eye. "Where'd they go?" And then they'll go about excusing why we disappeared. They'll have all kinds of theories and ideas of what happened to several million Christians who just vanished off the planet, but whether they see us go or whether we are just gone, it doesn't matter. The fact is we are going to end up before the throne of God. All the people who have been coming to church acting like Christians but who are just playing games are going to say, "Do you think that was it? Was that what they were talking about?" There are going to be a lot of people repenting, crying, and calling out to God when all the Christian folks have suddenly disappeared.

We do not know the day or hour of this event, but we do know the season. Look at Matthew 25:1-13: "Then shall the kingdom of heaven be likened unto ten virgins, which took their lamps, and went forth to meet the bridegroom. And five of them were wise, and five were foolish. They that were foolish took their lamps, and took no oil with them: But the wise took oil in their vessels with their lamps. While the bridegroom tarried, they all slumbered and slept. And at midnight there was a cry made, Behold, the bridegroom cometh; go ye out to meet him. Then all those virgins arose, and trimmed their lamps. And the foolish said unto the wise, Give us of your oil; for our lamps are gone out. But the wise answered, saying, Not so; lest there be not enough for us and you: but go ye rather to them that sell, and buy for yourselves. And while they went to buy, the bridegroom came; and they that were ready went in with him to the marriage: and the door was shut. Afterward came also the other virgins, saying, Lord, Lord, open to us. But he answered and said, Verily I say unto you, I know you not. Watch therefore, for ye know neither the

day nor the hour wherein the Son of man cometh."
Notice Jesus said, "I am coming." There is no question about that. "The Son of Man is coming, but you
don't know the day and you don't know the hour."
So that means *just be ready*. If you think you are
going to go out and sow your wild oats, do your
thing, have your fun, and then just before the rapture comes get saved, you might as well forget it.
You are going to miss out. "Well, I just want to find
myself." "Well, I just want to go over and have one
last *good* time." I can guarantee that will be your
last good time. That's what happened to the five
foolish virgins.

There are those who take that parable to say
there are some Christians who won't go in the rapture. Christians who are filled with the Holy Ghost
and are on fire for God will go in the rapture, but
Christians who are just playing around and not
doing too much for God will not go in the rapture. If
that was true, it would be teaching us that those
who work hard will go to heaven and those who
don't will not. We might as well start handing out
magazines and collecting dimes and start earning
our way to heaven. That concept is just not true.
You are not going to heaven because of your works.
You are going to heaven if you are a new creature
through faith in Christ Jesus. When you get there,
those who haven't been doing anything will not
receive any reward, and those who have been obeying the Word of God will be rewarded accordingly.
The correct meaning of the parable is there are
some who have received the Spirit of God and when
Jesus comes they will enter into heaven. Those who

have not been born again, who have not accepted the new birth, who have not made Jesus their Lord, will be shut out and will have no part in the rapture when He returns. Luke 12:32-40 says: "Fear not, little flock; for it is your Father's good pleasure to give you the kingdom. Sell that ye have, and give alms; provide yourselves bags which wax not old, a treasure in the heavens that faileth not, where no thief approacheth, neither moth corrupteth. For where your treasure is, there will your heart be also. Let your loins be girded about, and your lights burning."

Does that mean you should never turn your light out when you go to bed? No, that means be ready, always be ready. "And ye yourselves like unto men that wait for their lord, when he will return from the wedding; that when he cometh and knocketh, they may open unto him immediately. Blessed are those servants, whom the lord when he cometh shall find watching." That means He will find you ready. You won't say, "Now, wait, Lord. Before the rapture, let me just repent here for five or ten minutes. Let me say I'm sorry for all the things I've been doing that I know I shouldn't have been doing." If you are doing something you know you shouldn't be doing, you'd better stop it right now. "He shall gird himself and make them to sit down to meat, and will come forth and serve them. And if he shall come in the second watch, or come in the third watch, and find them so, blessed are those servants. And this know, that if the goodman of the house had known what hour the thief would come, he would have watched, and not have suffered his house to be broken through. Be ye therefore **ready** also: for the Son of man cometh at an hour when ye think not.''

Notice that last phrase, ''The Son of man cometh at an hour when ye think not.'' Now, you know in the midst of wars and inflation and depression and famine and confusion everybody says, ''Now is the time Jesus is coming. The world is so terrible. Things are so bad.'' Remember, back in World War II they all had it figured out that Mussolini or Hitler was the Antichrist. World War II was the worst destruction the world had ever known. ''This is the end. Jesus is coming soon.'' Everybody was ready for the rapture. That guarantees it wasn't going to happen then because He said He is going to come when you ''think not.'' In other words if you think in the natural that this is the time Jesus should come, then that's not it. When things are bad and everybody is scared and you think, ''Man, Jesus has got to come,'' that's not the time.

Later we are going to find out more about that time, but I want you to plug into that phrase, ''The Son of man cometh at an hour when you think not.'' That tells me He is going to come at an hour when everything is going good, when things are fired up. ''I don't need to get raptured when things are going good.'' That's when He is going to show up. That might sound a little strange to some of you, but as we go through some scriptures I am sure you will pick up on it. Look at I Thessalonians 5:1-8: ''But of the times and the seasons, brethren, ye have no need that I write unto you. For yourselves know perfectly that the day of the Lord so cometh as a thief in the night."

Most Christians stop reading right there and say, "Well, you know, the day of the Lord comes as a thief in the night, and we are never going to know when. It could be right now." If you read the Word, there are a lot of things that have to take place that haven't happened yet, so the rapture could not happen right now. I don't say that to discourage you. That is just a fact. He is coming for a glorious church, and we have a long way to go to become glorious. We have bits and pieces of a glorious church, but we still have a long way to go. He is coming for a church without spot or wrinkle. (Ephesians 5:27) We have a lot of ironing still to do on this earth! "For when they shall say, Peace and safety; then sudden destruction cometh upon them, as travail upon a woman with child; and they shall not escape." Notice he says the word *"them."* He didn't say "us," but *"them."*

"But ye, brethren, are not in darkness." That means it will not come upon *you* as a thief in the night, and *you* will not be in destruction, and *you* will have a way of escape. *You are not in darkness.* "Brethren" simply means those in the church, male and female. "But ye, brethren, are not in darkness, that that day should overtake you as a thief." So now when somebody says, "Well, you know, the day of the Lord comes as a thief in the night," all you have to say is, "Not as far as I am concerned. For the world, yes. The world will not know. They will be completely overtaken and surprised, but for me it won't be as a thief in the night. I'm not a child of the dark. I am a child of the light."

"Ye are all the children of light, and the children of the day: we are not of the night, nor of darkness. Therefore let us not sleep, as do others; but let us watch and be sober."

We need to be ready, be serious. This Christian life is not a joke. A lot of people who come to Christian Faith Center get uptight because we are talking about every nitty gritty thing. They are more interested in nice, cute, religious things that make them feel good. Nice and cute is not what Paul is talking about. He said you need to watch and be sober. This is serious business. This life is not a joke. Christianity is not something you try on for size. It's a life style. "For they that sleep sleep in the night; and they that be drunken are drunken in the night. But let us, who are of the day, be sober, putting on the breastplate of faith and love; and for an helmet, the hope of salvation. For God hath not appointed us to wrath, but to obtain salvation by our Lord Jesus Christ."

Think about this. Paul is saying you are not in darkness; you will not be unaware. Jesus has already told us we won't know the day or the hour, but Paul said you won't be in darkness and you won't be unaware. So what he is saying is that we will know the season. We will know the season and the general time when the rapture is about to happen. You and I will begin to sense it within our inner man. Remember, we have the Spirit of God within us, that the day is approaching, that the hour is drawing nigh, and we will be ready, sober, watching for the day to come. We won't know the exact day, and we won't know the hour, but I just wonder if as we are going up in the rapture we won't turn to one another and say, "I thought this was going to be the day. Oh, I just had a feeling that this was going to be it."

Now, if you look around the church as a whole, there is a general shaking going on. Preparation to meet the Lord is taking place, preparation for the final days on earth. There are all kinds of people getting involved with the Bible, all kinds of people who are realizing they need to get right with God. Some folks who have been in denominational churches for 40 years are getting born again, baptized with the Holy Ghost and speaking in new tongues. People who have had Bibles sitting on their coffee tables since they were three years old are starting to open them up to find out what it says. There is a shaking in all areas of life because that day is approaching. I don't think it will be in one month, one year, or even ten years, but it is getting close. I believe it will be within our lifetime. That could be 40, 60, or 100 years. I don't know how many years, but we are getting close. Paul said he was close, and that was 2000 years ago. We must *really* be close now. We don't know the day or hour of this event, but we know the season. We'll sense it in our own hearts as we get closer and closer to that day. When this catching away does take place, we shall receive new, glorified, spiritual bodies. Aren't you glad you have a new body coming? Look at I Corinthians 15:35-40: "But some man will say, How are the dead raised up? and with what body do they come? Thou fool, that which thou sowest is not quickened, except it die: And that which thou sowest, thou sowest not that body that shall be, but bare grain, it may chance of wheat, or of some other grain."

In other words, when you plant a seed, you are not expecting to receive seed when it grows up. You expect a plant of some kind. So the illustration means when you and I die, are buried, and are raised up, we will not receive the same kind of bodies that we have now. "But God giveth it a body as it hath pleased him, and to every seed his own body. All flesh is not the same flesh: but there is one kind of flesh of men, another flesh of beasts, another of fishes, and another of birds." That verse is a good verse for the evolutionists. There is one kind of flesh for man. He didn't grow up from the apes or the birds or the worms or the polliwogs. God created every thing with its own body. "There are also celestial bodies, and bodies terrestrial: but the glory of the celestial is one, and the glory of the terrestrial is another." In other words, on this earth we all have a body like Adam's, but there is coming a day when we will all have a body like Jesus's. Go on to verse 49: "And as we have borne the image of the earthy, we shall also bear the image of the heavenly. Now this I say, brethren, that flesh and blood cannot inherit the kingdom of God; neither doth corruption inherit incorruption." In other words, you are going to have to get a new body to be a part of the kingdom of God. "Behold, I shew you a mystery; We shall not all sleep, but we shall all be changed." Not everybody will die before the rapture takes place, but everybody will be changed into a heavenly or a glorified body. The Spirit of

God in you will change you in the twinkling of an eye, and you will put on an incorruptible body. You will put on a glorified body. You will have a new heavenly body just that fast, leave this earth suit behind and put on a heaven suit!

Now, for those who do not believe, who are not born again, they will remain on earth to live on through the tribulation and other events. If you miss the rapture, you are not forever doomed to hell. If you miss the rapture, it was not your last chance. What that means is you missed the best chance. People who do not go with the church in the rapture will have another opportunity, but I certainly would not want to go through the events to come.

There are many questions and there is much fear in people about whether the tribulation comes before or *after* the rapture of the church. For those of you who have read the book of Revelation, you will notice that the rapture of the church comes before the opening of the seven seals and the seven vials. It comes before the destruction and the wrath that is to be poured out upon the earth. So the evil that takes place during the tribulation period comes after the rapture of the church, but I just want to comfort you if you have heard a lot of doom and gloom and have a lot of fear and worry about what is going to happen in the end. Have no fear! If you are born again, you will be spared, delivered, and caught away from all the destruction that will happen on the earth.

The seven years after the rapture, known as the tribulation, will be a time of training for the church and trouble for the earth. A lot of times we don't explain words we use, and people get confused. There are tribulations that you and I go through on this earth today. If you talk to some Russian Christians, they will say they are in tribulation right now. If you talk to some people in the church who are fighting with sickness or lack of jobs, they will say they are in tribulation right now. That's true. There is tribulation we go through and have to endure and overcome. And yet there is a time of tribulation that is far greater than any tribulation people experience today. There is coming a time when there will be more confusion and there will be more evil control throughout the earth than you and I experience today. The tribulation we talk of today is really not comparable to the great tribulation that will last for approximately seven years. Instead of going through the tribulation, we will celebrate the marriage supper of the Lamb and then prepare for the millennium. Let's read Revelation 19:7-9: "Let us be glad and rejoice, and give honor to him: for the marriage of the Lamb is come, and his wife hath made herself ready. And to her was granted that she should be arrayed in fine linen, clean and white: for the fine linen is the righteousness of saints. And he saith unto me, Write, Blessed are they which are called unto the marriage supper of the Lamb. And he saith unto me, These are the true sayings of God."

So you understand, this is talking about you and I here because we have the righteousness of God. We are the saints. During the tribulation, the Antichrist will be loosed on the earth and much destruction will take place. Now, the Antichrist is not Satan. The Antichrist is a man Satan has trained and is following the devil. He will have power enough to take control over approximately ten nations during his reign on earth.

During the first three and a half years of the tribulation, the Antichrist will appear to bring the earth to a place of peace and harmony. It will look like a one-world religion, a one-world system, a one-world government, and one-world money is really working well. But in reality chaos and destruction will be being prepared. The whole thing will be getting ready to explode in the Antichrists face.

There are some things I want you to realize. The Antichrist is not going to rule the whole world. He will not track everyone down who won't take the mark of the beast and either cut their head off or kill them somehow. The Antichrist is not going to be so powerful that there will be no choice but to submit to him. He will only rule about ten nations of the earth. It is generally accepted that those ten nations are what is called the Commonwealth in Europe right now. A couple more nations will join up very shortly, and it will be ten nations. That excludes Africa, Asia, North America, and South America. If you will study carefully, the Antichrist never controls total power over any of those continents. He has a certain amount of power over those ten nations, but even within them there is much rebellion against him. He never takes control over Asia because there is a great army that will come down from China to fight him. He never takes control over the United States because the U.S. is talked about as being a nation that comes to help Israel. So the Antichrist is not an all powerful, all-world-ruling being. He is the most powerful thing that the devil can come up with, but you all know Satan's track record.

Because of negative thinking, some Christians like to find something to be scared and worried about. We have taken the Antichrist and made him a great big giant who would rule the whole world and scare everybody to death so that we would have something to worry about. Somebody got a bill from a department, and it said, "666." "Oh, the Antichrist got a hold of that company." Somebody built a computer over in Brussels, and they call it The Beast. "Oh, it has to be the Antichrist." The Antichrist is not a computer. He is a man. The Bible says the Antichrist is a homosexual. I have never seen any homosexual computers. (You can find out about that in the book of Daniel if you do a little digging.) Don't blow the Antichrist out of proportion. He is the devil's best shot, but the devil really doesn't have too much success. The Antichrist will be loosed on the earth, and there will be a great deal of destruction that will take place during the tribulation. Let's go on to II Thessalonians 2:1-3 and read from the Amplified Bible: "But relative to the coming of our Lord Jesus Christ, the Messiah, and our gathering together to [meet] Him, we beg you, brethren, not to allow your minds to be quickly unsettled or disturbed or kept excited or alarmed, whether it be by some [pretended] revelation of [the] Spirit or by word or by letter [alleged to be] from us, to the effect that the day of the Lord has [already] arrived and is here. Let no one deceive or beguile you in any way, for that day will not come except the apostasy comes first—that is, unless the [predicted] great falling away of those who have professed to be Christians has come—and the man of lawlessness (sin) is revealed, who is the son of doom (of perdition)."

Notice there is a man of lawlessness, and that is who we call the Antichrist. Any time you have a concept of lawlessness, you have no control. The devil has never been able to get any organization together because his whole concept is based on rebellion. So he even rebels against those who are rebelling. The world rebels against itself. The world can't get in agreement on anything. I want you to see that the Antichrist is not going to take over the whole world and have a world government that controls everything. He is never going to have that much power. He is always going to have trouble.

Two of the greatest troubles he will have will take place about half way through his rule. He is going to set up shop in the city of Jerusalem, and two prophets are going to show up. These two prophets are from God. About the time the Antichrist announces himself ruler of the world and tries to set himself up as God, they are going to stand up and say, "You are a liar." The Antichrist will send his men, and on international TV (the Bible said the whole world is going to see it) they are going to try to kill the two prophets. The prophets will just speak "fire" and burn them all up. They will be turned to ashes. Here the Antichrist has just announced he is God, and he already has two prophets he can't handle. His reputation gets blown right away. You can read about the two prophets in the book of Revelation. Let's look at II Thessalonians 2:3 in the King James: "Let no man deceive you by any means: for that day shall not come, except there come a falling away first, and that man of sin be revealed, the son of perdition."

Now if you study that verse in the Greek you'll find it also has to do with a catching away or an escape, and it has reference to the rapture. The man of sin, the Antichrist, cannot be revealed until you and I get out of here. We are going to find many scriptures that teach us God cannot pour out wrath or judgment until His people are "out of town."

Now, let's say that the Antichrist did get revealed before the church left. What would we do? We'd all go to intercessory prayer. We'd start church wide prayer meetings every day of the week. We'd start having 500 to 1000 people coming out for prayer. There would be people all over the United States and other countries of the world interceding against him and his work. How much work do you think he is going to get done with all that going on? Whatever we bind on earth will be bound in heaven. Whatever we loose on earth will be loosed in heaven. According to the confession of your mouth, so shall it be. It is obvious he cannot be revealed until you and I leave. Verse 4: "Who opposeth and exalteth himself above all that is called God, or that is worshipped; so that he as God sitteth in the temple of God, shewing himself that he is God."

So you see that he tries to set himself as God over the earth. But notice in verses 5 and 6 that there is something holding him back: "Remember ye not, that, when I was yet with you, I told you these things? And now ye know what withholdeth that he might be revealed in his time." There is something that is keeping him from being revealed. What is that? The church, the body of Christ on the earth. We are the light holding off the darkness. We are the light of God pushing back the darkness of the devil. He can't be revealed until you and I are gone because we are withholding him.

He is going to have some miraculous powers, but they are all going to be lying wonders. They are all going to be deceptive. Let's move on to verses 8 through 10: "And then shall that Wicked be revealed, whom the Lord shall consume with the spirit of his mouth, and shall destroy with the brightness of his coming: Even him, whose coming is after the working of Satan with all power and signs and lying wonders, and with all deceivableness of unrighteousness in them that perish; because they received not the love of the truth, that they might be saved." He is going to be a master at the art of deception. He is going to be well developed and well trained at deceiving and lying, and it is all under the inspiration of the devil. But God is going to consume him with the spirit of his mouth. He will, however, deceive many, and people who follow him will not receive the truth and will not be saved.

Yes, people can be saved during the tribulation and the millennium. After the tribulation, there is going to be a war of Armageddon, and a lot of battles will be going on. The climax of all this is the return of the Lord Jesus Christ with you and me right behind Him. The Bible said He is going to come riding on a white horse. On His thigh will be written the Word of God. He will come out of heaven to take control over the whole planet. Jesus will return after seven years, and you and I will be with Him in our glorified bodies.

The devil will have his armies all gathered together in Armageddon. The armies of Asia will be coming to fight against the Antichrist's armies. When they realize that Jesus is returning, both the Antichrist and Asian armies are going to gather together and fight the armies of Jesus. Of course, you know how long that is going to last! Within just a few minutes, we will wipe out all of the enemy's armies. They will be completely destroyed. The Bible talks about blood running up to the horses' bellies. All people who fight against Jesus will be immediately wiped out.

Jesus will then walk into Jerusalem through the same gate that He walked out of. He'll set up His throne in the temple, and He will rule over the earth, the Bible says, "With a rod of iron." What that means is whether you like it or not, you will submit to Jesus. In Philippians 2:10, 11 it says: "That at the name of Jesus every knee should bow, of things in heaven, and things in earth, and things under the earth; and that every tongue should confess that Jesus Christ is Lord, to the glory of God the Father." Now, you can do it willingly as a servant, or you can do it because He is going to rule with a "rod of iron."

During that time, we will enter into what is called the millennium. Jesus will rule and reign on this earth for 1,000 years. There will be perfect peace. The lions will lie down with the lambs. Animals that used to fight will become partners together. Animals that used to eat meat will become vegetarians. The whole world will just be at peace. The whole planet will be completely controlled though the Lordship of Jesus Christ. You and I in our glorified bodies will reign with Him on earth. We will have different places around the world we are in charge of.

In Matthew 25, the Bible talks about being faithful over little and He will make you a ruler over much. In one parable, He gave the man cities and countries to rule over. So it may be God distributes to His people countries and cities over which they have control. Some will be servants and helpers. Others will be mayors. Others will be governors and presidents. How do you know what you are going to be? By what you do right now. If you're just messing around right now, then He is probably going to have you take the garbage out for the collectors during the millennium. But if you will be faithful in what you are doing right now He will make you a ruler over much during that time.

God's wrath which will be poured out during the tribulation will be toward His enemies, not the church. II Corinthians 5:21 says: "For he hath made him to be sin for us, who knew no sin; that we might be made the righteousness of God in him." What can God judge if you are righteous? He can't pour

His wrath out on His own righteousness.

There are stories about God's judgment on the earth in the Old Testament. Look at Genesis 7 and the flood which Noah was involved with. God could not begin the rain until Noah and all who were righteous were in that ark. God shut the door to make sure they would be safe and the rain would not affect them. When the judgment came down, the Ark went up, and they were above that destruction and were not affected by it. Noah went around preaching for over 100 years before the flood to try to get more people to join him, and they laughed at him. They said, "You are a nut. You're building a boat, and there isn't even any water around here. You have flipped out, Noah." But his seven children went into that boat, and they were all spared.

Then in Genesis 19 you have the story of Sodom and Gomorrah. God, because of the evilness and wickedness of that city, judged that city unworthy to continue on. But what happened first? He sent angels in to get all that were righteous. Lot had to leave with his family before judgment could come. In Nahum 1:2 it says: "... The Lord will take vengeance on his adversaries, and he reserveth wrath for his enemies." You are not an enemy of God, so He can't pour His wrath out on you.

God's wrath, through the tribulation and destruction, goes out to His enemies. You don't have to worry about that stuff. As long as you are a believer and want to follow the Lord and you are made the righteousness of God in Christ by being born again, you will be spared from all that destruction. I Thessalonians 1:10 says: "And to wait for his Son from heaven, whom he raised from the dead, even Jesus, which delivered us from the wrath to come."

At the end of the millennium, Satan will be loosed for a season. There are still some who will choose to follow him. They will make one last attack on Jerusalem and the Lordship of Jesus. Jesus then will end that war for the last time. Satan and all of his followers will be cast into the lake of fire for eternity. You and I then will be on the new earth with the New Jerusalem and the new heaven, and we will live that way for eternity.

HAVE YOU BEEN BORN AGAIN?

The first step to a successful Christian life is that you be born again. The Bible says in John 3:3, "... Except a man be born again, he cannot see the kingdom of God." Every person must be born again to know God and have everlasting life.

Being born again is making a commitment. It is making Jesus the Lord of your life, your master, teacher, and guide, to change from your ways to follow Jesus (Romans 10:9-10).

Just say this simple prayer: "God, I come to you in the name of Jesus. I ask you to come into my life. I confess with my mouth Jesus is my Lord, and I believe in my heart you raised Him from the dead. I thank you I am saved. Amen."

You are now born again! You are forgiven of your sins and on your way to heaven. This is just the beginning of a new life. The Bible tells us in Romans 12:2 to renew our minds: "And be not conformed to this world, but be ye transformed by the renewing of your mind, that ye may prove what is that good, and acceptable and perfect will of God."

Send for my book *Living the New Life.* This book will help you understand more about the new life you have chosen. Let me hear from you!

Is there a special need in your life? Do you need prayer? Casey Treat Ministries has an intercessory prayer team, and we will pray for you. Please let us know your need, whatever it may be, and send it to:

Casey Treat Ministries
P.O. Box 98581
Seattle, Washington 98188
206 824-8188

ANOINT WITH OIL: To place oil, generally on a person's forehead. A means given by God to release His healing power into another person. James 5:14

ANTICHRIST: A great opponent of Jesus who will spread evil throughout the world, who will be defeated when Jesus Christ comes back to earth at His second coming. I John 2:18,22

ANGEL: A supernatural being, either good or bad which has greater than physical power. They are spirit beings. They do not have human bodies but can assume human form when necessary. Hebrews 13:2

ARCHANGEL: The highest ranked of all angels. Jude 9, I Thessalonians 4:16

BIBLE: The Bible is the collection of 39 books of the Old Testament and 27 books of the New Testament bound together. It is the divinely inspired record of God's revelation of Himself and His will for mankind. II Timothy 3:16, Hebrews 4:12

BISHOP: An overseer. A bishop in the New Testament is also referred to as an elder. They are to have oversight of the spiritual affairs of the church. I Timothy 3:1

BODY: Man is a three part being: spirit, soul and body. The body is the flesh or material substance in which the spirit and soul of the man resides. I Thessalonians 5:23, I Corinthians 3:16

BORN AGAIN: To be born again is to experience the creative, life-giving work of the Holy Spirit. He regenerates those who are dead in sin so that they are quickened or made alive spiritually and are changed from being the children of the devil to becoming the children of God. When a person is born again they become a child of God and have a relationship with Him. Romans 10:9, John 3:3

CLEAVE: To join fast together. To cleave to your husband or wife would be to leave your separate families and join together with each other to make your own home and family, to become as one. Genesis 2:24

CORPORATE WORSHIP: A group or body of believers praising and worshipping God together. Worshipping God at the same time and at the same place. It is shared by all members of the group. Psalm 107:32, II Chronicles 5:13-14

COVENANT: A binding and solemn agreement made by two or more individuals to do or to keep from doing a specified thing. It is a promise or undertaking either human or divine. Luke 1:72,73

DEVIL: One of the names of Satan. Also referred

to as the fallen angel. He is the chief evil spirit working against God. He perverts all good to produce evil and keep men from God. Matthew 12:24, I Peter 5:8

DISCIPLE: One who believes in and follows Christ. An imitator of Christ. John 8:31

FAITH: Unquestioning belief, and conviction based upon hearing, that does not require physical proof or evidence. Hebrews 11:1

GENTILES: All people other than Jews or the nation of Israel. During Bible times, a Gentile was a heathen or someone who did not worship God. Acts 9:15

GRACE: Unearned, undeserving favor. Kind, forgiving, or compassionate treatment toward others. Romans 3:24

HOLY: Belonging to or coming from God. To have a holy life is to live a pure, clean life, avoiding sin and evil. Romans 12:1

IN THE GREEK: The Old Testament was translated in Greek before the birth of Christ. The New Testament was originally composed in Greek. We reference to the Greek to get the most literal translation or meanings to words.

INSPIRATION: An influence from God upon human beings. Could be creative thoughts or actions. The Bible was inspired of God. II Timothy 3:16

INTERCEDE: To stand in the gap for someone else. To plead or make a request in behalf of someone else or others. Ezekiel 22:30

KING JAMES: The revised English translation of the Bible published in England in 1611 with the authorization of King James I.

KINGDOM OF GOD: All who are born again and acknowledge Jesus Christ as Lord of their life. They are willingly submitted to God's rule and authority and are in fellowship with Him. Matthew 18:1-4

MERCY: A response of love and kindness not based upon actions or conditions. To show love and compassion though it has not been earned or deserved. Jeremiah 3:12

MESSIAH: One of the names used to describe Christ. It means "The One promised of God as the Great Deliverer." The Messiah was the expected saviour or deliverer of the Jews. Daniel 9:25, Isaiah 9:6

MILLENNIUM: A thousand year reign by Christ on the earth during which time Satan is bound and will have no influence on the earth. Revelation 20:2

PENTECOST: In the Old Testament it was basically a harvest festival. In the New Testament, Christ rose from the dead as the first to be resurrected and 50 days later the Holy Spirit was poured out upon men. Acts 2:1

PHARISEE: A member of an ancient Jewish group of people who strictly observed the written law and traditions, and believed that all people should do the same. Luke 11:39-44

PROPHET: A person who speaks under divine inspiration and revelation from God. He does not teach what he has learned or studied but speaks what God gives or shows him directly. Ephesians 4:11,12

RAPTURE: The believers will be removed from the earth by Christ, and caught up to meet Him in the air. Matthew 24:31,40

REPENT: To acknowledge and change wrong actions, thinking; sin. Luke 15:7

RESPECTER OF PERSONS: One who passes judgement on people and categorizes them. They do not see all men and women as equal or the same. James 2:3

RESURRECTION: The raising up of Christ from the dead. Rising up from the dead and coming back to life. Luke 14:14, I Thessalonians 4:15-17

RIGHTEOUS: To be in right standing with God. God sees us as being "just," without prejudice or partiality. I Peter 3:12, Romans 5:19

SALVATION: Deliverance. We were delivered from the bondage of sin, sickness and disease, and poverty when Jesus died for us. He took all those things upon Himself so that we could be saved from them. John 3:16

SOUL: The soul is made up of our mind, emotions, and will. The soul has no physical or material reality, but is credited with the functions of thinking and willing; therefore, determining all behavior. Hebrews 4:12, I Thessalonians 5:23

SPIRIT: The spirit is the activating force within human beings. It gives life to the body and lives on when the body is dead. It is the life center. I Thessalonians 5:23, Proverbs 20:27

THE WORD: The Bible. God's inspired Word given to man. II Timothy 3:16

TITHE: One tenth of your income or what you produce, that is to be given back to God. Proverbs 3:9, Malachi 3:10

TONGUES: The supernatural gift of speaking in another language without its having been learned. It is also referred to as "praying in the spirit." Acts 2:4, I Corinthians 14:2

Books by Casey Treat

God's Financial Program
Living the New Life
God's Word for Every Circumstance
How to Receive the Baptism With the Holy Spirit
Renewing the Mind: The Arena for Success
Your Vision Is Your Future
The Power Is In You
You Can Have a Prosperous Soul
You Make the Difference
Fulfilling God's Plan for Your Life
Setting Your Course
Living a Transformed Life

Available from your local bookstore.

For a complete catalog of books and tape series by
Casey Treat, write to:
Casey Treat
P.O. Box 98581
Seattle, Washington 98188

HARRISON HOUSE
P. O. BOX 35035
TULSA, OK 74153